T0354271

Seeing Red

Platform Studies
Nick Montfort and Ian Bogost, editors

Seeing Red

Nintendo's Virtual Boy

José P. Zagal and Benj Edwards

The MIT Press   Cambridge, Massachusetts   London, England

The MIT Press would like to thank the anonymous peer reviewers who provided comments on drafts of this book. The generous work of academic experts is essential for establishing the authority and quality of our publications. We acknowledge with gratitude the contributions of these otherwise uncredited readers.

This book was set in Helvetica Neue and FilosofiaOT by Westchester Publishing Services. Printed and bound in the United States of America.

Library of Congress Cataloging-in-Publication Data

Names: Zagal, José Pablo, author. | Edwards, Benj, author.
Title: Seeing red : Nintendo's Virtual Boy / José P. Zagal and Benj
    Edwards.
Description: Cambridge, Massachusetts : The MIT Press, 2024. |
    Series: Platform studies | Includes bibliographical references and index.
Identifiers: LCCN 2023034670 (print) | LCCN 2023034671 (ebook) |
    ISBN 9780262045063 (paperback) | ISBN 9780262361842 (epub) |
    ISBN 9780262380669 (PDF)
Subjects: LCSH: Nintendo video games—Design. | Video games—Desgin. |
    3-D video (Three-dimensional imaging) | Virtual reality.
Classification: LCC GV1469.32 .Z34 2024 (print) | LCC GV1469.32 (ebook) |
    DDC 794.8/3—dc23/eng/20230920
LC record available at https://lccn.loc.gov/2023034670
LC ebook record available at https://lccn.loc.gov/2023034671

10 9 8 7 6 5 4 3 2 1

Contents

Series Foreword

How can someone create a breakthrough game for a mobile phone or a compelling work of art for an immersive 3D environment without understanding that the mobile phone and the 3D environment are different sorts of computing platforms? The best artists, writers, programmers, and designers are well aware of how certain platforms facilitate certain types of computational expression and innovation. Likewise, computer science and engineering have long considered how underlying computing systems can be analyzed and improved. As important as scientific and engineering approaches are, and as significant as work by creative artists has been, there is also much to be learned from the sustained, intensive, humanistic study of digital media. We believe it is time for humanists to seriously consider the lowest level of computing systems and their relationship to culture and creativity.

The Platform Studies series has been established to promote the investigation of underlying computing systems and of how they enable, constrain, shape, and support the creative work that is done on them. The series investigates the foundations of digital media—the computing systems, both hardware and software, that developers and users depend upon for artistic, literary, and gaming development. Books in the series will certainly vary in their approaches, but they will all share certain features:

- a focus on a single platform or a closely related family of platforms
- technical rigor and in-depth investigation of how computing technologies work

- an awareness of and a discussion of how computing platforms exist in a context of culture and society, being developed on the basis of cultural concepts and then contributing to culture in a variety of ways—for instance, by affecting how people perceive computing.

Acknowledgments

I don't have a good "origin story" for how I came to be interested in the Virtual Boy (VB). I had no awareness of it until the mid-2000s and then, as far as I can recall, I heard about it and started buying stuff on eBay. As many scholars often do, I then thought it would be fun to write a paper about it (the Virtual Boy, that is, not my eBay shopping). To help me out, I somehow recruited the brilliant, then undergraduate student Matt Zachara. We poked around in the hardware, he introduced me to the (not currently recommended) oven-fix for glitchy display repairs, and we wrote and published "Challenges for Success in Stereo Gaming: A Virtual Boy Case Study." That's where the story should have ended.

Except that, in 2009, Nick Montfort and Ian Bogost published *Racing the Beam*, a platform study for the Atari 2600. I love that book. I recall talking to Ian at the Game Developers Conference at around that time and suggesting a platform study on the Virtual Boy. My (bad) pitch was that there were so few games that you could write about all of them! Ian smiled, said something akin to "Sure, send us a proposal," and the rest would have been history. Except that it took me forever to send a proposal. When I did, it wasn't good. It took even longer for me to send a better one. And it's taken even longer to write the book itself.

It has been about fifteen years, and I've been embarrassing myself for almost that long talking about how I'm working on a book about Nintendo's Virtual Boy. I should say "working" with air quotes though because it has been a battle—mostly against myself—to make any progress despite always wanting to work on it. My experience with this book is not one of those where the world acts against you and you succeed despite all odds. It's mostly been a tale of procrastination, working on other things instead because they seemed more urgent or important, of continuously saying to myself, "I'll work on this next week when I have some more time," and next week it turns out I don't have the time. And so on. Through all this I've been lucky. Lucky to have had support from the institutions I've been at—DePaul University first, from whom I was able to get funding and support for translations and travel, and later from the Division of Games at the University of Utah. I've been lucky that Ian Bogost and Nick Montfort, the series editors, have been patient with me—prodding and poking along the way such that the flame stayed alive. Lucky in the quality of the feedback received along the way from anonymous reviewers as well as friendly colleagues (thanks anonymous reviewers, Pawel Grabarczyk, Mariana Amaro, and many more). I've been lucky for the broader communities of people dedicated to collecting, preserving, and sharing video game–related materials. This includes, but is not limited to, the Video Game History Foundation and the incredible resource that is the Internet Archive. I was fortunate in being able to support John Szczepaniak's work interviewing Japanese game developers that later became his amazing *The Untold History of Japanese Game Developers* books, an important source of until new information about the development of a handful of Virtual Boy games. I was also lucky in convincing a then complete stranger (to me), Benj Edwards, to embark with me on a promise that neither fame nor fortune would likely result of this collaboration. Most of all, I have been lucky that the Virtual Boy fan community is incredibly supportive, active, welcoming, and determined to do the best it can to preserve, maintain, discover, support, and continue to build on a platform that is maligned and ridiculed to this day. Christian Radke (KR155E), Kevin Mellott, Guy Perfect, DogP, Morintari#9416, blitter, and many more whose names and handles I forget, it is on the shoulders of your work that this book stands—thank you!

—José Zagal
September 2023

***

Writing a book about the Virtual Boy nearly thirty years after its demise is an interesting thing. Many people have never played one and don't realize how it could be important or interesting in the history of video games, but I think we've put together a compelling view of why that might be the case. I am thankful to my coauthor, José Zagal, for inviting me to undertake this multi-year journey with him. He did most of the work and deserves most of the credit. Harry McCracken also deserves mention for editing my Virtual Boy history piece that I pitched to *FastCompany* in 2015. Thanks to the Virtual Boy veterans at Reflection Technology for talking to me back then. Also, I'd like to thank Jeremy Parish for supporting my harebrained joystick ambitions by commissioning my first Virtual Boy joystick, the BX-250, that I built in 2018. He also loaned me a Virtual Boy flash cart so I could test it out with every game, which also allowed me to develop the BX-240 Hyper Fighting joystick. And Jeremy's Virtual Boy Works book, where I provided a screenshot gallery, is a great addition to video game history. Screenshot outtakes from that gallery process came in handy for this book. I'd also like to thank Kevin Mellott for sending me a Hyper32 flash cart so we could play every Virtual Boy game again accurately on original hardware, which allowed us to write the Appendix. Stay hungry and stay virtual, my friends.

—Benj Edwards
September 2023

What's in a name? In the case of the Virtual Boy, a lot.

The size and cultural significance of the video game industry has grown dramatically since the early days when arcade machines ruled supreme. This growth has provided financial and creative opportunities that have drawn the interest of many individuals and companies as they have carved out their own spaces within the industry. Many succeeded, but perhaps many more have failed. Of all the failures the games industry has witnessed over the years, perhaps the most famous—or infamous—is the Virtual Boy.

Nintendo released the Virtual Boy, a red-and-black standalone table-top video game console that featured stereoscopic 3D graphics, in mid-1995. The firm quickly discontinued it in 1996 after disappointing sales and lackluster critical reception. The Virtual Boy's red-only graphics proved prophetic, echoed soon after by red ink on Nintendo's ledgers.

Why was the Virtual Boy a commercial failure? Many have wondered why it failed and what we might learn from this (e.g., Boyer [2009]; Zachara and Zagal [2009]; Edwards [2015]). Was it doomed because it was not powerful enough to compete with the other game consoles of its day? Perhaps, despite running on batteries and its association with Nintendo's popular handheld Game Boy device, consumers were disappointed that it wasn't portable. Or it could be that, because it had a stereoscopic display and a helmet-like chassis, consumers expected it to be something it was not, that is, an affordable standalone virtual reality (VR) system for video game play. The Virtual Boy featured neither head-tracking nor motion-tracking input. In fact, given its stationary nature, you could not move your head around at all. Ironically, for a platform predicated on its ability to provide players with a novel way of perceiving things (stereo 3D), the public's perception of the platform did not align with its capabilities.

In this volume, we will explore Nintendo's Virtual Boy platform. Examining the reasons for its failure is an obvious thread that we will tug on a little. However, we will also show that this is neither the only reason to examine the Virtual Boy nor, arguably, the most interesting.

As Nicoll (2019) argues, "Although the media archaeological moment has led to a richer and more comprehensive engagement with video game history, it has also contributed to a tendency to fetishize rather than critically account for failure and marginality" (17). We agree with Nicoll, and, in this context, we will show how Nintendo's Virtual Boy:

1. builds on and extends a historical tradition in immersive, visually engaging entertainment that was largely unexplored in video games at the time;

2. has a softography of games with a distinct shared visual aesthetic style that has not been significantly developed nor explored since the Virtual Boy's release, having been superseded by polygonal 3D graphics; and

3. is a compelling example of how a platform's meaning lies as much in its design and technical capabilities and affordances as it does in an audience's perception of those capabilities or lack thereof.

It is the third bullet point that is, in fact, the central theme of this book—the background questions that motivated it include wondering about how we think of video game platforms, what they are and how they help us perceive a game's gameworld, and what might that mean in the context of the Virtual Boy—a device for which misperception is central. Its stereoscopic displays provide the illusion, not the reality, of depth, and its commercial disappointment is also contextual. As Nintendo icon Shigeru Miyamoto admitted, had it been marketed and sold as a novelty toy rather than a video game platform, its resulting approximately 770,000 units sold would have led to its perception as a commercial success (Iwata 2011). "I thought we needed to treat it like a niche product" (Miyamoto, in Iwata 2011).

What's to Come

This book neither provides a chronological review of the Virtual Boy's hardware and softography nor is it an examination of Nintendo. Similarly, this book is not a history of virtual reality, or even virtual reality–adjacent systems. Rather, it is a Virtual Boy platform study (Bogost and Montfort 2007; 2009)—an in-depth examination of a platform including its technical capabilities, the games that were created for it, and the technocultural context of the United States in the 1990s in which it was released. While the Virtual Boy was also officially released in Japan, we will not examine this context specifically.

We will discuss and examine many, but not all, of the games released for it—highlighting those games we have found particularly useful for illustrating the arguments we wish to make. That being said, we do include a brief overview of the platform's complete softography of the Virtual Boy's twenty-two commercially released games in appendix B. Readers interested in more detailed information on each of the games can refer to Jeremy Parish's excellent *Virtual Boy Works* (2021). Similarly, there is Jeffrey Wittenhagen's *The Complete Virtual Boy*, notable for its thorough[1] coverage of homebrew Virtual Boy games, including those released as physical cartridges with custom boxes and labels (2019).

The Virtual Boy's key feature was its stereoscopic technology—it featured two displays (one for each eye) and provided a realistic illusion of depth. In chapter 2, we broadly examine the role of stereoscopy in entertainment media—the illusion of seeing something as three-dimensional when what is being viewed is not. We primarily focus on visually immersive entertainments such as boardwalk electromechanical arcade machines and early video games that used "viewports." The viewport was a way to create visually immersive experiences designed to focus a viewer's attention and minimize distractions (e.g., reducing peripheral vision). They also tantalized with the promise of something interesting to look at.

We will also discuss the idea of seeing things differently and how that has been implemented in amusements for the masses and portrayed in popular media. In this sense, the Virtual Boy connects to two traditions in entertainment media: (1) the creation of devices for altering our visual perception (what we see) and (2) peering into devices to view artificially created worlds. So, while the Virtual Boy was not unique in providing a stereoscopic experience, it was trying to provide something different: a new kind of gameplaying experience.

The origins of this promise for new kinds of video game play experiences lie both in the technology at the heart of the Virtual Boy as well as the design philosophy of its creator, Gunpei Yokoi. In chapter 3, we discuss the history and provenance of the Virtual Boy's display technology and articulate the potential that Yokoi saw in that technology. Namely, Yokoi was interested in creating new kinds of experiences because he felt that the audience for games should be broader and that current TV-based video games had reached their limits.

We also articulate how the Virtual Boy aligned with Yokoi's design philosophy: "lateral thinking with withered technology" (Makino 2010b). This philosophy broadly consists of exploring alternative and interesting uses for well-established inexpensive technology. The Virtual Boy's display technology, licensed from the US company Reflection Technology, used inexpensive red LEDs that provided creative and commercial opportunities.

We examine some of these in chapter 4 by discussing the affordances the Virtual Boy has for displaying graphics and how, contrary to what many assumed, its strengths lie in manipulating and presenting 2D graphics (e.g., tiles, sprites, and backgrounds) rather than the polygonal 3D graphics that were starting to become popular at the time the Virtual Boy was being developed. In addition to explaining how the stereoscopic illusion is achieved, we outline three techniques used by Virtual Boy game creators to create sophisticated tile-based stereoscopic images: flat element stereo (billboards), stereo-within graphical elements, and aggregate-element stereo.

In chapter 5, we examine how the graphical affordances described in chapter 4 are implemented in the Virtual Boy's commercially released softography. Many Virtual Boy games have a distinctive visual signature that goes beyond its red graphics. We call this signature aesthetic the "layered diorama," and it appears in most of the Virtual Boy's games.

The layered diorama aesthetic is one where the player experiences (looks at and plays in) a miniature boxed game environment (the diorama) whose elements, rather than being fully three-dimensional, are instead flat (two-dimensional). The flat elements are placed at different distances from the viewer, thus constituting the layers of the layered diorama. We show how the layered diorama builds on earlier representational traditions including the peep boxes of the seventeenth century and techniques developed for animated film in the early twentieth century. Virtual Boy is thus a development of the peep box but with the addition of digital computational technologies that allowed for motion, increased variety of images to look at, and, perhaps most importantly, meaningful user interaction.

Chapter 5 also includes an overview of the main ways that the layered diorama style is implemented in different games. We note a few distinctions—for instance, we see games in which the style is limited to background or decorative elements with no impact on gameplay. There are also arguably more sophisticated implementations of the style, where gameplay occurs across multiple layers and these interact with each other in nontrivial ways.

The layered diorama visual style prevalent across many Virtual Boy's games—especially those developed internally by Nintendo—represents a natural progression from ideas tentatively explored in earlier titles for Nintendo's Super Nintendo Entertainment System platform. This represents a clear example of incremental innovation in game design afforded by technological (in this case graphical) affordances of a given platform. We can only speculate as to what this innovation might have looked like had the Virtual Boy been on the market for a longer period of time and benefitted from more games being developed for it.

Conversely, given the game industry's transition at the time toward a different paradigm for implementation of on-screen graphics (Järvinen 2002)—polygonal 3D graphics replacing the use of flat tiles/sprites—Virtual Boy's game design explorations in multilayer gameplay might not have had much impact even if the platform had remained commercially viable for a longer period of time.

Having established how the platform operated and what its games looked like, we turn to how it was perceived by consumers and the media. In chapter 6, we examine the role that Nintendo's marketing efforts played in creating different perceptions of the platform that ultimately contributed to the general public being both confused as to what kind of a platform the Virtual Boy was and how to make sense of it.

The Virtual Boy's launch coincided with a moment in time during which there was much confusion and uncertainty about the direction (or directions) of the video game industry. This was what Nicoll (2019, 14) calls a "moment of rupture." Established product categories (arcade, console, portable, and personal computer) were starting to shift, and new questions emerged: Was VR going to become a new product category for video games? The personal computer had multimedia CDs and better graphics, but now consoles with similar affordances were becoming available. And, what about "cyberspace"? Online connectivity was starting to disrupt how games were played, sold, and distributed. Ultimately, we argue that Nintendo failed to establish a strong perception (and identity) for Virtual Boy as a platform—for some it's a console, for others it is an inadequate portable or a lackluster virtual reality device. This lack of clear identity, or platform misperception, continues long past the platform's demise as the Virtual Boy is regularly used as an example of a failed virtual reality device in children's (e.g., Martin [2018, 8–9]) and popular media books (e.g., Simons and Newman [2018, 214]).

While we argue in chapter 6 that the public's perception and misperception shaped our understanding of the Virtual Boy as a platform in ways that were detrimental to its success, perhaps the public got it right all along and it was all style with no substance. We entertain this hypothesis by exploring the following question: Was the Virtual Boy a gimmick? We examine this question in chapter 7 by using Ngai's (2020) *Theory of the Gimmick* as a framework for exploring the nature and meaning of gimmicks in video games. The video game industry has always relied on, and made use of, gimmicks as a means to sell both hardware and games. Nintendo was no stranger to this strategy as it showed with its toy robot R.O.B.—the gimmick that helped get the Nintendo Entertainment System (NES) video game system onto the retail shop floor and from there into the living room (Altice 2015; Ryan 2011).

Thus, we examine whether or not the Virtual Boy, as a platform, should (or could) be considered a gimmick. We consider Nintendo's intentions for the console, how well (or poorly) it was supported, and how it compares to other hardware released at around the same time. Ultimately, we find that Virtual Boy's reputation as a gimmick appears to postdate the console's release, tracing it to a time when it was used as a cautionary tale when considering newly announced hardware such as the Nintendo DS—that is, is it a gimmick because of its two screens, one of which is a touchscreen?

We hold that it is not reasonable to consider the Virtual Boy, as a platform, a gimmick. However, in the second half of chapter 7, we examine whether its key feature, stereoscopy, should be considered thus. Again, we rely on the video game media press to get a sense of when a feature is considered a gimmick or not. We find that the key indicator of "gimmickness" as a pejorative is when the feature has a negative effect on gameplay or is perceived as ancillary to the game's central experience. To answer whether stereoscopy is a gimmick, we examine two titles, *Virtual Boy Wario Land* (Nintendo R&D1 1995b) and *Red Alarm* (T&E Soft 1995c), and we look at how reviewers at the time described the games' use of stereo 3D. For *Wario Land*, we find that stereo 3D is used in a way that reinforces and strengthens the game's central gameplay theme: movement between foreground and background. Thus, it is not a gimmick, as the game is improved by the feature. *Red Alarm* is a stronger case since, in practice, the game is mostly unplayable without stereoscopy. This can be easily verified directly since the game allows players to adjust how much depth the displays should emulate—including the option for no depth at all. In sum, we find that considering stereoscopy in games as a gimmick, while possible for some titles, is not a given. The Virtual Boy includes at least two titles for which this feature was a significant part of its core gameplay or was required in order to have a reasonable play experience.

Finally, in chapter 8, we wrap up by considering what has happened in virtual reality and stereoscopic gameplay since the Virtual Boy was released. Here, we focus on the present perceptions of the Virtual Boy.

We do this in two parts. First, we examine the activities of the Virtual Boy fan community. Then we briefly look at how the platform has appeared in Nintendo's games since it was canceled.

Unlike other retro video game fandoms, the Virtual Boy community is less defined by nostalgia and more closely aligned with an inherent curiosity for the platform that often results in attempts to imagine an alternative past, one in which the Virtual Boy was afforded the possibility of achieving its potential. This potential, cut short by Nintendo's rapid cancellation of the Virtual Boy, has mostly focused on creating, locating, and releasing things that "should" have been released in the first place. This includes the Virtual Boy GameLink cable designed to make use of the existing communication port that allows for two Virtual Boy units to communicate with each other. This functionality was then implemented in a fan-made *Street Fighter II* clone (called *Hyper Fighting*) game that plausibly could have been released by Capcom at the time. Multiplayer play was also restored in *Mario's Tennis*, a Virtual Boy launch title, from unused code found by disassembling the game's code. Further efforts have focused on locating, restoring, and releasing games that were canceled shortly before they were to be launched. These titles are seen by many as games that could have "turned the tide" for the Virtual Boy as they were part of a second wave of releases that never happened. Because the Virtual Boy did not have the benefit of a regular product lifecycle, Virtual Boy fans perceive that the Virtual Boy was never fully realized as a platform, and their work goes a long way toward "redeeming" the public's perception of it.

Our examination of how Nintendo has used the Virtual Boy since it was canceled shows something similar. Over the years, Nintendo has slowly warmed to its commercially failed platform, and it has acquired a small measure of cultural capital as it appears in the background of other games or becomes an in-game collectible to be sought after. It is now a quirky and fun part of Nintendo's history as it is referenced and left for those "in the know" to recognize. It has even been used in a self-deprecating fashion— perhaps in an attempt to seem "cool" as virtual reality devices have become popular. As with the fan community, there is a renewed perception of the Virtual Boy as something quirky and fun that illustrates how perceptions of a platform are fluid and that the perception can sometimes matter more than what it actually does, how it works, and what games were released for it.

As mentioned earlier, we have also included an appendix with brief descriptions of each of the Virtual Boy's officially released titles as well as an appendix with some of the technical specifications for the platform. But for now, time to start seeing red.

In 1838, a year before the birth of practical photography, Charles Wheatstone presented a device to the public. He had been working on it for a few years, and it was accompanied by a paper. The paper, which explained his ideas and findings on how human binocular vision worked, also included a collection of drawings designed to be viewed using an apparatus he invented (Wheatstone 1838).

And so, the stereoscope, a device that used a pair of mirrors and two specially prepared pictures to provide the viewer with the illusion of viewing a three-dimensional object, made itself widely known.

There's a clear link between the stereograph, the name commonly given to the images viewed through the stereoscope, and the Virtual Boy. Both are technologies that allow the illusion of seeing an image as if it has depth, which allows three-dimensional perception. However, there is a second, perhaps stronger, link that connects the two inventions: people's desire to trick their eyes for the purposes of entertainment and wonder.

It did not take long for Wheatstone's device to move from the realm of science into the upper-class parlor where it became a source of amusement and entertainment (Fleckenstein 2016). Shortly thereafter, it would take the United States (Wajda and Grover 1992) and the rest of the world by storm.

It seems curious that the stereograph should precede photography, but the truth is that we have long been drawn to and fascinated by the activity of looking at things that surprise, amuse, and entertain us. We have similarly been drawn to altering the act of looking itself—finding ways to visually experience things differently, either through illusion and trickery or by changing the context of viewing.

In this chapter, we will briefly examine the history of stereoscopy in entertainment leading up to the release of the Virtual Boy. We will also discuss the idea of seeing things differently and how that has been implemented in amusements for the masses and portrayed in popular media. The Virtual Boy appears in this broader context as it connects to two traditions: (1) the creation of devices for tricking our eyes, thus altering what we see, and (2) the creation of devices we peer into to view artificially created worlds.

Devices for Altering What We See

According to Darrigol (2012), humans have speculated on the nature of light and vision since the middle of the first millennium BC, and optical wonders such as rainbows, shadows, and reflections have captured our interest for as long as we can tell.

This fascination—to understand how light and vision work—has always been accompanied by the creation of artifacts that help us see the world differently. For example, Seneca is said to have written how "letters, however small and indistinct, are seen enlarged and more clearly through a globe of glass filled with water" (as quoted in Bradbury [1967]).

The Arabian scholar Ibn al Haitham (better known as Alhazen) studied lenses and their effects on light and vision. His work would later lead to the development of spectacles in the thirteenth century. By the sixteenth century, lens-making existed as an industry, and with it came years of experimentation and study that led to the proliferation and development of microscopes, telescopes, and other devices designed to enhance, augment, and subvert the act of viewing (King 1955).

These devices mostly remained in the hands of the rich and learned, and it was not until the nineteenth century that, perhaps as a result of the development of cheaper forms of manufacturing and a middle class with money to spend, the use of optical devices for entertainment and diversion would spread far and wide. It is during this period that "philosophical toys" were developed—devices that were designed for study but also provided natural amusement (Wade 2004). As Gunning (2012, 500) notes, "These devices manipulate (many sources would describe it as fooling or tricking) human perception into seeing an image, thus creating visual experiences dependent on operating the devices." These toys included the kaleidoscope (Brewster 1858)—a tube containing loose bits of colored glass or plastic and mirrors placed in such a way as to create beautiful colorful symmetrical patterns that change as the tube is rotated or shaken. Many more would be invented and developed, including the polyorama panoptique, the stereo-scope, and the alethoscope. They all required looking through something for the desired effect to be achieved.

This tradition of creating devices for seeing things differently continues to this day. In addition to telescopes and kaleidoscopes, we also have physical tools and devices such as night-vision goggles, View-Master toys, and low-cost virtual reality goggles like Google Cardboard or Nintendo's Labo VR Kit. These devices have also been recreated in the virtual and digital world. For example, video games often allow players to diegetically see virtual environments differently by simulating the existence of such technologies or devices. In first-person shooter games, for example, weapons might have a telescopic scope that can be peered through to provide a closer view of objects that are far away. In military-themed games, players are often able to "turn on" night-vision, seeing the world through the lens of simulated light amplification, or, as made famous by the 1980s action movie *Predator* (McTiernan 1985), "heat vision"—in which things seen on screen are depicted in bright colors corresponding to their (supposed) temperatures. Digitally, the possibilities are endless with creators experimenting with ways to allow people to see the world through different or augmented eyes in ways that may not be possible technologically currently (or ever).

As a platform, the Virtual Boy was simply another embodiment and extension of this desire and interest. It is a device that promised a different way to see things in a game: stereoscopic 3D. However, the Virtual Boy was neither the first (nor last) time that stereoscopy would be used in games.

A Brief History of Stereoscopy in Videogames

The Virtual Boy, as a standalone video game device for stereoscopic 3D play, is not a historical anomaly. Rather, it is part of a long tradition of gadgets and devices designed to see things differently.

Over the past four decades, game designers have achieved stereoscopic effects in a variety of ways. However, we need to consider both the video games (as software products) and the hardware necessary (if any) to achieve said stereoscopic effect. As such, there are games that:

1. are not stereo friendly (this is most games)
2. provide alternate modes or configurations such that they can be played in stereo
3. were designed/created with stereo in mind (e.g., cannot be played/viewed properly on a regular screen).

In terms of hardware, numerous techniques and approaches have been developed or invented over the years with varying degrees of quality in terms of the overall viewing experience. Broadly speaking, however, we can distinguish:

1. peripherals for existing game devices or systems
2. devices that are nonelectronic
3. standalone electronic hardware devices.

In 1982, GCE released one of the earliest peripherals for stereoscopic play, the 3D Imager for its Vectrex console. The 3D Imager consists of a pair of goggles with a special spinning disc mounted in front of the eyes. As the disc spins, it blocks vision from one eye at a time. By synchronizing the disc's rotation with the display of images on the screen that were designed to be viewed by a specific eye, the illusion of depth is created. GCE only released three games for use with the 3D Imager: *3D Crazy Coaster*, *3D Mine-Storm*, and *3D Narrow Escape*.[1]

Another notable example is the SegaScope 3D Glasses released by Sega for the Sega Master System (SMS) console in 1988. This peripheral was designed to look like wraparound sunglasses. Here, the 3D effect was caused by a "shutter system": the left and right liquid crystal lenses would alternately darken and lighten in synchronization with the images displayed on the TV screen. Sega published four stereo SMS games that required the glasses: *Blade Eagle 3-D*, *Space Harrier 3-D*, *Maze Hunter 3-D*, and *Missile Defense 3-D*. Three games marketed as "3-D" also included a 2D mode playable without the glasses: *Out Run 3-D*, *Poseidon Wars 3-D*, and *Zaxxon 3-D*. Finally, *Line of Fire*, while not advertised as a 3D game, included a 3D mode that could be activated separately.

There are also examples of games with an alternate viewing mode that required a nonelectronic hardware device. In 1987, Square released *Rad Racer*, *3-D World Runner*, and *JJ*. Each came bundled with a pair of anaglyph glasses. Anaglyph glasses consist of two color filters, usually red and cyan. The filters are used to separate colors on a superimposed anaglyph image, enabling each eye to see an image slightly offset from the other, thus providing the perception of depth. Another example is Konami's *Metal Gear Acid 2* (2005) for the Sony PlayStation Portable (PSP). This game came bundled with a folding cardboard box with two eyeholes that needed to be placed over the handheld. When the game is switched to a special mode, the game displays two images on either side of the PSP screen (one for each eye) producing a stereoscopic effect. This technique is like that employed by Google with its Google Cardboard VR attachment—essentially a fold-out cardboard viewer with embedded 45 mm focal length lenses.

Independent hardware devices for stereo video gaming are perhaps the rarest examples. These devices all require games that are specially designed with stereo video in mind (though they might be playable on a regular screen under certain conditions). Nintendo's Virtual Boy is probably the most notable, though there are earlier examples. For instance, toy manufacturer Tomy released a series of at least seven handheld 3D gaming devices starting in 1983. Each was a single-game unit that resembled a pair of binoculars with buttons on the top of the device. The devices contain an LCD display that generates two images that are directed to each viewport using an internal optical pathway (Hamano and Matsumoto 1985) to produce a stereoscopic effect.

Today, we have reached a point where "designing for stereo 3D" is perhaps no longer necessary. For instance, 3D video card manufacturer Nvidia allows users to configure the settings of some of its video cards to output stereo video (viewable with 3D shutter glasses). The video card, which processes the information ultimately displayed on the screen, is able to directly modify the video data to generate an image that is different from what the game would normally display. Thus, the player can view the game in stereo video even though the game doesn't support that viewing mode natively (thanks to additional drivers). Therefore, stereo 3D is not as exotic as it once was—in some cases, it's just another viewing mode that, with the appropriate hardware, can simply be switched on or off.

The previous examples are by no means an exhaustive list of games, peripherals, technologies, or techniques. However, they illustrate how stereo video is something that electronic games have toyed with for a long time using a variety of technologies. None of these examples, however, was able to achieve what could be called significant mass-market success.

This continues to be true even as there have been significant advances in technology, price, and consumer adoption of stereoscopy in video games. In the post–Virtual Boy years, it is perhaps VR and auto-stereoscopic devices (such as the Nintendo 3DS) that have seen the widest adoption.

Of the more recent VR headsets, Sony's PlayStation VR, PlayStation VR2, and Meta's (formerly Facebook) Quest (formerly Oculus) devices deserve the most accolades for bringing VR to a large audience for the first time. The PlayStation VR, a peripheral device for the PlayStation 4 that had, as of January 6, 2020, sold five million units (Sony Interactive Entertainment 2020), has been a huge success in terms of install base. However, this pales in light of the total number of PlayStation 4s sold. Facebook's Oculus devices are not far behind: the Oculus Quest 2 headset, designed to work as a standalone headset or be hooked up to a desktop computer, saw the end of 2020 with highest sales ever recorded for a non-smartphone-related VR device (*Edge* 2021).

Nintendo's 3DS console released in 2011 is another strong contender for "mass market success." The device's novel feature is its auto-stereoscopic display that can display stereoscopic 3D effects without additional hardware or the need for users to wear special glasses. The stereo depth effect can be adjusted or even turned off by moving a slider along the side of the screen without the need to restart the device or reboot a game. The system was well received at launch, and Nintendo had sold approximately seventy-six million units worldwide as of December 31, 2021, across its different hardware versions of the system (Nintendo 2021). It is also worth noting that Nintendo later released the Nintendo 2DS and New Nintendo 2DSXL, both of which lack the stereoscopic functionality.

As we have shown, the Virtual Boy is not particularly unusual or special as a device for stereoscopic 3D play. There was both an earlier tradition of devices and peripherals as well as a later one. However, this tradition is not the only one the platform was connected to.

Devices We Peer into to View Artificial Worlds

While people were busy understanding lenses and inventing devices to see things differently, there was also a parallel effort and drive in experimenting with neat things to look at. In the seventeenth century, Dutch painters developed "perspective boxes." A perspective box is an empty wooden box that contains painted pictures on its inside walls—usually representing the interior of a building (Verweij 2010). The device contains a window to let in light and a peephole for viewing. When the viewer looks through the window on the front of the box, everything seems odd and distorted. However, if you look through the peephole instead, everything comes together in a surprising way: you are now gazing into a miniature world whose interior space seems larger than the box.

The peephole and the lens, combined, gave birth to the experience of peering into a new world.

Residents of Venice created a similar box called the *Mondo Nuovo*. Thanks to the clever use of lenses, candles, and even mirrors, it allowed people to view specially created images of celebrations and historic events. These devices, often presenting images in varying light conditions, were intended for use by one person at a time (Campagnoni and Pacini 2016). They were both voyeuristic as well as escapist. They let "spectators project themselves into a dimension of total illusion and venture out on a virtual journey through times and places far distant from their present" (Campagnoni and Pacini 2016, 24). Mondo Nuovo devices came in a wide variety of shapes and sizes, from large boxes you had to lean into to peer through small viewports on the side to smaller devices you would hold up to your face like a pair of binoculars.

Some of the more elaborate Mondo Nuovo devices contained miniature worlds consisting of a series of images, drawn or printed, that artists cut out and placed in a succession of layers inside the device such that they offered the viewer a three-dimensional scene. More sophisticated constructions allowed for different scenes via changes in the lighting (night and day being a common transition) and by moving or replacing some of the cut-out images (Ogata 2002). Many of these peep boxes also used perspective, mirrors, and other techniques to convey depth and an illusion of spatiality beyond the confines of the box (Zone 2007).

The development of the stereograph, and photography soon after, furthered interest in these peephole devices. One notable innovation would be the kinetoscope—a device allowing a single person to view a moving image by peering through a peephole window at the top of the device. For the kinetoscope, the novel thing to look at was a short film reel of something interesting—for example, a man sneezing in slow motion or Annie Oakley firing a rifle at glass balls.

While not strictly for stereoscopic vision, the Mondo Nuovo devices, or peep show devices, as they are more commonly referred to in English, are an early technology designed to create a new, virtual world and to immerse the participant in that experience via a carefully curated visual experience. The peephole defines and alters what the viewer can see while simultaneously providing a new and interesting vista to experience. And while the visual delights of the Mondo Nuovo devices were often historical, biblical, or geographically inspired, it is not hard to see that representing the fantastic and imaginary were obvious next steps. In a way, the Mondo Nuovo devices were an early form of what we would now call virtual reality.

Achieving the desired effect—transporting the viewer into the scene before them—was not easy to implement. The design of the scenes themselves was of course important, but there were other factors. In his 1895 stereoscope patent, H. C. White (1895, 1) describes one such challenge: "As the common hand-stereoscope has heretofore been made the hood has only been made to fit the upper part of the face, leaving the space below the plane of the eyes of the observer open, so that much light from below would find access to the eyes, which more or less interferes with perfect vision in using the stereoscope." White's solution to the problem of interference from outside light was to modify the "hood" such as to create "a practical camera obscura between the face of the observer and the lens frame when the stereoscope is applied to the face in actual use" (White 1895, 1). The aesthetic goal was not just to allow the viewer to see something special but to also provide them with a sense of wonder and presence. As Zone (2007, 20) notes, "The experience of looking into a private space, as with a keyhole, shut out everything but the enclosed image. This visual exclusion of the world might have provided a sudden notion of revelation, as if exposing something that might have been hidden."

The desire to want to be inside another world, without actually having to be inside it, has persisted over the years. The kinetoscope was essentially a movie theater inside a box that required peering through a peephole viewer window on the top. These peephole devices would also extend to amusements and games—first electromechanical, then digital.

For example, in 1966, Sega released one of its first arcade games, *Periscope*. In this electromechanical game, players look through a simulated submarine periscope and aim and fire torpedoes at cardboard ships mounted on a chain that moves across the field of view (Horowitz 2018). Here, the "peephole" is the periscope—a novelty that would prove commercially successful and would see other electromechanical imitators such as Midway's *Sea Raider* (1969) and *Sea Devil* (1970) games. The periscope-as-peephole would continue with video games such as Midway's *Sea Wolf* (1976), Atari's *Battlezone* (1980), and Grand Productions's *Up Scope* (1986). The submarine gameplay initially made successful in *Periscope* was even remade by Sega in *Subroc-3D* (1982).

Subroc-3D is considered the world's first commercial stereoscopic arcade video game. Here the "periscope," a unique binocular viewport, generated a stereoscopic effect via two half-clear, half-opaque spinning discs—one per eye. The discs spun in synchronization with images on the monitor so that, while an image for the left eye showed on the screen, the right eye's view was blocked by the opaque portion of a disc, and vice versa with the right eye. The stereo 3D effect was the result of "a combination of parallax and the after-image effect of the spinning discs" (Horowitz 2018, 53).

While Sega was working on the original 1960s *Periscope*, two parallel developments were taking place. First was Morton Heilig's Sensorama (patented in 1962). The Sensorama was a semi-enclosed arcade machine you sat in to watch movies in stereoscopic 3D—it was like sticking your head inside a box. But it also included stereo sound, fans for blowing air, smell generators, and a vibrating chair (Burdea and Coiffet 2003). Heilig developed and created several films/experiences for it, including one that provided "a surprisingly convincing illusion of riding on a motorcycle" (Delaney 2014). The Sensorama did not see mass market success and is perceived by some as a "dead end" in terms of technology and entertainment. However, it is perhaps fairer to view it as a development ahead of its time that attempted to create a novel and more immersive way of experiencing movies.

The second development that paralleled Sega's *Periscope* was Ivan Sutherland's work on computer-based virtual reality. Sutherland, a professor of computer science at the University of Utah, worked on developing technology "that would allow people to interface with computers by being inside 3D computer graphics" (Furness 2014). Rather than stick your head into a device, what if you strapped the device to your head? While there were a few earlier devices similar to Sutherland's, his head-mounted display (HMD) system was novel in that it allowed the wearer to see simple computer-generated graphical objects floating in front of their eyes (Sutherland 1968). The system, which in one implementation was suspended from the ceiling, was able to track the wearer's head movements and alter the computer-generated image seen accordingly (Sutherland 1968). These devices, precursors to what we now call virtual-reality headsets, allowed for the generation of real-time images, a significant leap from either static or prerecorded images, as well as responsiveness to user input.

Virtual reality would continue to be developed by Sutherland and many others throughout the 1970s and 1980s in university laboratories and military research groups interested in computer graphics, simulations, and "super cockpits" for military vehicles.

Virtual reality as a technology and a concept would not enter the public consciousness until two things happened.

First, Howard Rheingold's book *Virtual Reality* (1991) helped popularize the term "virtual reality." Rheingold (1991, 16) articulated a vision for this new and exciting technology: VR made it possible to "immerse yourself in an artificial world and to reach in and reshape it." Thanks to miniaturization, improvements in computer processing speed and capacity, and advances in simulation and computer graphics, it was finally possible to consider wider adoption of VR. It was also this time when, as Rheingold (1991, 67) notes, VR was able to bring together interests from both computer science and entertainment: "VR is neither strictly a child of computer science nor a form of entertainment, but something that necessarily partakes of both technical legacies."

Second, the Hollywood movie *The Lawnmower Man* (Leonard 1992) provided a visualization for what a VR experience could be. While the movie was generally panned by the critics, it found a following and was moderately successful at the box office. The movie was notable for its (at the time) groundbreaking and extensive use of computer-generated imagery. "More importantly, the film introduced the concept of VR to a wide audience" (Kirby 2011, 215).

While Rheingold's book explained what VR was, it was something hard to understand without the benefit of direct experience. This is where *The Lawnmower Man* succeeded: the movie "visualized an abstract concept in such a way that its potential was immediately understood" (Kirby 2011, 221). The movie presented a future vision that extrapolated on what was currently available and showed how this new technology could be used for entertainment, education, spiritual development, and even sexual activity. The VR technology shown in the movie "created a 'modern myth' that whet the public's appetite for enhanced VR and immersive entertainment technologies" (Kirby 2011, 226). The movie allowed the general public, largely unaware of what VR was, to imagine what video games could be. The hype for VR had begun.

Fortunately, consumer-facing VR entertainment experiences were already available. The earliest was the Virtuality system developed by W Industries and launched in 1991. The system had two main configurations, sitting down and standing up, and was intended for use in video game arcades. In both configurations, players would wear a virtual reality headset and use a handheld controller (or steering wheel and airplane yoke for some of the sitting-down units).

Each system configuration supported several different games, with the most popular and well-known being *Dactyl Nightmare* (Green 1999) for the stand-up configuration: "In *Dactyl Nightmare*, the objective of the game is to score points by 'shooting' other characters. The participants play across a game board suspended in space—five fields, connected on two different levels via staircases. A recurrent threat is a Pterodactyl which attempts to pick up, and drop (thereby 'killing') the players in the game" (Green 1999, 457). Other notable games were *Grid Busters*, *Hero*, and *Legend Quest*, this last one a collaborative role-playing adventure that allowed players to save their progress (Delaney 2014). Virtuality would continue releasing upgraded versions of its systems throughout the 1990s.

The 1990s would see the appearance of VR in video game arcades, museums, and galleries as well as the creation of dedicated VR centers (Green 1999; *Retro Gamer* 2007). While early VR experiences were considered expensive, "as a novelty, it [was] worth the bucks" (Keizer 1993, 12).

The reception among the video game press was perhaps more subdued. Craig Engler, writing in late 1992 for *Computer Gaming World*, notes how "For the first time anyone with a few dollars could go out and try virtual reality and, at least in the beginning, a lot of people did," but "the novelty of that particular system seems to have worn off" (Engler 1992, 80).

In practice, VR games had two problems when compared to non-VR video games of the time: the games were not as fun to play, and the graphics were not as good and were rapidly looking worse when compared with "regular" computer video games thanks to the appearance of 3D graphics acceleration (see chapter 6). Virtuality's *Legend Quest* had "noticeable lag in the response of the virtual environment to the user, poor graphics resolution, and other features which are of a relatively low technical standard" (Schroeder 1995, 50). Similarly, its *Zone Hunter* game was panned as "a depressingly familiar Doom-style first-person shooter" that was not "as good looking as Virtua Cop" even as "the [VR] medium is cool and full of potential" (*Next Generation* 1995c, 150); *Sega Pro* magazine noted that "graphically it lacks that final stroke of realism to put you in a Lawnmower Man-esque situation, but for [the price of] a credit, what do you expect?" (*Sega Pro* 1994, 9). As early as 1995, it was recognized that "few of the VR companies have produced titles that would even compete with the poorest of video games" (Gagnon Hawkins 1995, 184). It would seem that the success of VR up until that moment was due to the novelty of the equipment in an arcade setting rather than the quality of the experience.

While it is beyond the scope of this book to detail the rise and fall of the VR hype of the 1990s, it is important to understand that this is the context in which Nintendo developed and released the Virtual Boy console. The virtual reality companies were aware that their software was not as interesting to consumers as they imagined, so it made sense to reach out to video game companies. Similarly, video game companies were looking to VR as a potential future of video game entertainment. Even toy/game companies such as Hasbro explored and announced their own VR products (*Next Generation* 1995d). Nintendo was not the only video game company to work on what was perceived in the early 1990s as the next step in virtual reality entertainment—the home VR device. In fact, Nintendo might not even have been the first.

Nintendo's competitor, Sega, had been working on the Sega VR headset for use with its Mega Drive console since 1991 (Harris 2014). The headset featured a passive system for orientation tracking developed by VR company Ono-Sendai (Jacobson 1994, 95) and was demoed at several events including the 1993 Chicago Consumer Electronics Show (CES) in June (*Mean Machines Sega* 1993). Sega intended to release the Sega VR by the end of 1993, but it postponed the release to 1994 and then ultimately canceled the project entirely.

Virtuality, the leader in arcade-based VR entertainment, teamed up with Atari to produce a VR headset for the Jaguar console (*Next Generation* 1996). Atari announced the peripheral at the Winter 1995 CES. Atari reportedly completed the Jaguar VR unit, including a playable version of *Missile Command* in 3D, but never released the headset due to the Jaguar's poor sales (*Retro Gamer* 2007, 76).

Both the Sega VR and the Jaguar's VR headset were planned as peripherals to existing consoles. They also featured head tracking—something the Virtual Boy did not include. Curiously, they were styled using the same color scheme as the Virtual Boy: red and black.

The Virtual Boy: The Next Step in a Long Tradition

As we have shown, the Virtual Boy was far from being an "out-of-left-field" device. Rather, it was simply another example of a device intended for entertainment that built upon two long-standing traditions. The first tradition, the creation of devices for tricking our eyes to alter what we see, is manifested in the Virtual Boy through its use of stereoscopic vision: present each eye with a slightly different image to trick the brain into perceiving a flat image as having depth.

The second tradition, the creation of devices we peer into—for example, through peepholes that limit the interference of outside light—to view artificially created worlds, is manifested by the Virtual Boy's inspiration drawn from the VR systems and headsets of the time. Here, the artificially created worlds are dynamic and generated by computer hardware.

This lineage—from philosophical toys and peep boxes to video games—has not gone unnoticed. Sharp (2007, 279) notes how "The peep-box presented the Japanese with an interface made of glass, representing what was seen as a Western 'lens culture' (borrowing a term from Norman Bryson) and foreshadowing the video game interface of the glass monitor." Similarly, Gunning (2012) uses the term technological image to refer to those images produced by image-making optical instruments including magic lanterns. Gunning emphasizes the importance of interacting with these devices to both understand and be surprised by their manipulation of our senses. The technological image has perceptual novelty, and "describing the production of these images as a trick expresses the perceptual ambiguity they occasion without defining them as illusions or deceptions" (Gunning 2012, 510). These devices have a certain "magical" nature: through our interactions with them, we know how they work, yet we still enjoy their results.

However, the "magical" promise and nature of the Virtual Boy was not that of simply viewing images in 3D. Nor was it the promise of exciting games and entertainment. Ultimately, the Virtual Boy, as its name implied, was building off the promise of virtual reality to provide "an entirely new gaming medium rather than just a new game" (Engler 1992, 80).

Not much is publicly known about how Nintendo came to be interested in developing what would ultimately become the Virtual Boy. Was Nintendo committed to VR video games as a future for video games and looking for technological solutions that made business sense? Or was the Virtual Boy primarily the result of Nintendo going "off script" and seizing a unique, and possibly risky, opportunity that presented itself? The answer is probably a little bit of both. Also, what was the broader Japanese context in which Nintendo's considerations about VR were taking place?

In this chapter, we will show how, contrary to its reputation, the Virtual Boy was not an anomaly in Nintendo's history with video game platforms. Rather, it was the result of a deliberate strategy that was consistent with Nintendo's way of doing things and informed by its lead creator Gunpei Yokoi's design philosophy. We will examine three things: how Nintendo came to develop the Virtual Boy in the first place, Gunpei Yokoi's design philosophy and its influence on the platform, and what the platform's technology consisted of.

Nintendo Dabbles in Virtual Reality?

The late 1980s and 1990s were a heady time for virtual reality (see chapter 2), and, when it came to generating public interest, Japan was arguably leading the charge. In May 1991, Hattori Katsura's *Jinkō genjitsukan no sekai* (The world of the feeling of artificial reality) was published (Roquet 2022, 59). It was the first best-selling general audience book on VR, beating Howard

Rheingold's watershed *Virtual Reality* by a few months (Roquet 2022, 58–59). Japan is also "where VR was first repackaged as a consumer technology" (Roquet 2022, 9) and, by 1991, had more VR systems than anywhere else in the world (Roquet 2022, 11).

However, VR was neither presented nor perceived in the same way in Japan as it was in the United States. First, while VR research in the United States was largely developed and driven by military interests, in Japan, it came out of a telecommunications context (Roquet 2022, 53). Second, in the mid-1990s at least, Japanese VR research had an engineering emphasis rather than computer science like in the United States (Watson 1994). Thus, the Japanese public's perception of VR was shaped by the additional availability, via public demonstrations for example, of VR devices and experiences different from those shown elsewhere. These devices and experiences were characterized in the United States as "cool gadgets" and "strange experiments" (Lanier 2017, 216; Roquet 2022, 68) but would, perhaps taken together, provide alternative highlights of VR's potential as a medium. It was the Japanese who quickly understood VR as a means for providing novel sensory experiences that allowed for more immersive personal control over imaginary worlds. Specifically, VR provided the promise of a mediated alternative to everyday Japanese life (Roquet 2022, 11). As Roquet (2022, 7) notes: "In Japan, the headset's ability to block out the world becomes a primary feature rather than something to be disavowed. VR promises not just entry into another world but a way to perceptually bracket out the current one—and a user's place within it."

That being said, there is little firsthand evidence that demonstrates how everything that was happening in the VR space influenced Nintendo in the 1990s. However, prior to the release of the Virtual Boy, Nintendo designers and engineers expressed at least some interest in virtual reality. For example, when interviewed by Satoru Iwata about the development of the Nintendo's autostereoscopic handheld Nintendo 3DS, Shigeru Miyamoto commented that: "To start at the beginning, at the time [just before the creation of the Virtual Boy] I was interested in virtual reality, and was one of the staff that went on and on about how we should do something with 3D goggles. I didn't exactly twist his arm, but I would talk with Yokoi-san about how [3D] goggles would be interesting" (Miyamoto as quoted in Iwata [2011]).

However, not much is known outside of Nintendo if this interest led to in-house experiments or the development of prototype virtual reality systems. Some reports, mostly secondhand, do exist that there was some research taking place. For example, while researching an article about the

Virtual Boy for *FastCompany*, Benj Edwards interviewed Takefumi Makino, the biographer of Gunpei Yokoi and a friend of Yokoi's for a period near Yokoi's death in 1997 (2015). According to Makino, Nintendo experimented with virtual reality prior to creating the Virtual Boy, but they found the experience unsatisfactory.

Specifically, Makino describes that Nintendo thought that VR was too "realistic" to translate well to Nintendo's fantastic style of games that involved mushrooms, goombas, and high-jumping plumbers. He said:

> At the time, Virtual Reality had become a worldwide boom. Mr. Yokoi, then, began looking for ways to use VR in games. However, the conclusion was that VR was not suitable for Nintendo video games. This was because Nintendo's games created an "unrealistic world" on the screen, giving users a variety of experiences within that world (in a "realistic world" there isn't anybody who can jump as high as Mario, or mushrooms that make you bigger, right?). VR, for its part, was seen as creating a "realistic world" in a virtual space, and giving users simulated experiences within that space. Mr. Yokoi's conclusion was that VR should be used in utilitarian products and was not suited for games. (Makino 2015)

It's unclear, in the quote above, whether Yokoi was referring to what he had seen or experienced in the VR industry at large at the time or if he was referring to his knowledge of prototypes and technology developed either internally or at companies partnered with Nintendo.

Internally, for instance, Nintendo had earlier developed LCD shutter glasses as an accessory for its Family Computer Console (see chapter 2). Was this device abandoned internally, or were there attempts at further development by attempting to pair it with head-tracking technology?

Externally, Nintendo had a close relationship at the time with Argonaut Software (later Argonaut Games), which had created, and helped further develop, the Super FX chip for Nintendo's SNES platform (*Edge* 1994). This chip, included in select game cartridges, was a graphical accelerator that allowed for real-time 3D polygonal graphics that were otherwise not technically possible on the SNES (Arsenault 2017). Argonaut's approach was technically innovative at the time (Dettmer 2001) and led to Nintendo reportedly being interested in pursuing another hardware project with Argonaut (McFerran 2019).

In a 2019 interview with *NintendoLife*, Jez San, Argonaut's founder, described how the Argonaut/Nintendo joint venture company A/N

Software began working on the development of a "VR Machine" called the "Super Visor" (McFerran 2019):

> "We designed a very cool 3D graphics chip for it," San explains. "We started researching motion tracking and had a system that worked. Nintendo had introduced us to Texas Instruments, who had this novel concept of what, at the time, was called the DMD—Digital Mirror Display—but has since become DLP, which stands for Digital Light Processing. Instead of using liquid crystal pixels, the chip had little mirrors and the angle of mirrors can be altered. The chip had the full image on it; it was like half an inch big, and it had a full 320 by 200 pixels on it. You shined lights on it—like red, green and blue lights—and you waggled the mirrors in software, and you'd get a display. We were going to use this display for the VR headset, and they had just invented this technology. It wasn't publicly known, so we were non-disclosed by Texas Instruments, and it would have been very cool." (McFerran 2019)

Nintendo reportedly invested a million US dollars on the device, which also included motion tracking, before deciding to pull the plug (McFerran 2019). However, unlike other unreleased devices from that time (e.g., Sega's unreleased VR headset, see *Sega Visions* [1993]), there is no physical or documentary evidence to date for the "Super Visor" (e.g., prototypes, photographs, or videos) or, perhaps more importantly, evidence demonstrating how close the device was to being a commercially viable product.

According to San, the project was canceled because Gunpei Yokoi preferred another display for use in a new Nintendo device—the display that would ultimately appear in the Virtual Boy (San quoted in McFerran [2019]). The timing is unclear, however. Jez San's comments suggest that Nintendo was simultaneously working on two "VR" devices: the Super Visor and what would become the Virtual Boy. Did the Virtual Boy's development begin prior to, or after, work began on the Super Visor? Was it the case that different groups were working on a Nintendo VR device unaware of each other, only for the Super Visor to be canceled due to Yokoi winning an internal political struggle? Perhaps the Super Visor was canceled simply because the Virtual Boy was further along in development such that there was clarity regarding its final cost and its possibility of shipping at a date that was convenient for Nintendo [i.e., as soon as possible, to maintain interest before the Nintendo 64 (N64) shipped]?

Hiroshi Yamauchi, Nintendo's president at the time, was known to encourage teams within Nintendo to compete against each other. Famously, Nintendo's research and development was initially handled by three (later four) competing divisions called Nintendo R&D1, Nintendo R&D2, and Nintendo R&D3 (Sheff 1993, 38–40; Ryan 2011, 65–66). Thus, it is plausible that Nintendo had two "VR" projects running simultaneously.

Regardless of the murkiness in this matter, a key technology that sparked Nintendo's Virtual Boy development was not made via Argonaut but rather through a US company that was not a part of the video game industry.

The Scanned Linear Array

The development of the Virtual Boy's hardware began with the creation of a high-resolution portable display called the scanned linear array (SLA), invented by Reflection Technology of Waltham, Massachusetts in 1986 and patented soon after (Becker 1990). The SLA used a one-dimensional vertical column of LEDs and a rapidly oscillating mirror to create the illusion of a two-dimensional rectangular display. This is the key piece of technology that made the Virtual Boy possible.

Reflection Technology founder Allen Becker invented the SLA because he wanted to create a small, high-contrast heads-up display for use with a portable computer. After several years of development, Becker and his team of engineers integrated the SLA technology into a commercial product called the Private Eye that was prototyped by late 1988 (Reflection Technology 1988) and ready for shipping in April 1990 (Engst 1990). The Private Eye was essentially a tiny computer monitor that the user positioned over one eye for a private, heads-up computer display that could serve as a portable replacement for a desktop cathode ray tube (CRT) monitor or portable LCD on a conventional IBM PC compatible of the time. The Private Eye could simulate the view of a twelve-inch display seen eighteen inches away, but it had a catch: it could only display shades of red.

The SLA used red LEDs because Becker discovered a source of single-line LED assemblies used in the large-format drum printer industry. Red LEDs had been in production since 1968 and were a mature and inexpensive technology—something that, as will be discussed later, aligned well with Gunpei Yokoi's design philosophy.

Reflection Technology engineer Ben Wells described why they used red LEDs in a 2015 interview with Benj Edwards:

The way a laser printer works is you have a sheet of semiconductor material. It's usually a drum, and the laser—if you could see with my hand—I'm shining a light back and forth on the drum. You slowly rotate the drum, and the laser traces out the image. The toner sticks to [the drum], and all you need is something that will cause the static charge on the drum to dissipate, and it turns out red light is the trick.

That's why there were red LEDs. If the world had invented blue LEDs before red, then it would have been blue instead. (Wells 2015)

While today it might be possible to construct a full-color LED display similar to the Private Eye using red, green, and blue LEDs, it wasn't practical in the 1980s or early 1990s. Inexpensive, reliable, high-powered blue LEDs weren't commercially available until around 1994—slightly too late for the Virtual Boy (Lin 2014; NobelPrize.org 2014). According to Ben Wells, Reflection Technology never developed a color version of the Private Eye display (Wells 2015).

Selling the SLA

While seeking a wider market for its SLA display invention, Reflection put together a virtual reality video game demo circa 1990 using two Private Eye displays, one for each eye, that were mounted to a welder's mask (Wells 2015). They added head-tracking and linked it to a portable PC that ran a first-person tank game they either developed in-house or licensed from others—Reflection staff's memories were unclear on this point during interviews. The tank game displayed a first-person view from a tank window and allowed the player to shoot other tanks.

Reflection unsuccessfully pitched their tank-based VR demo to toy and video game companies including Mattel, Hasbro, and Sega. Sega in particular worried that the technology could cause motion sickness (Kalinske 2015). In 1991, Reflection offered the display to Nintendo where it caught the attention of one of Nintendo's top inventors, Gunpei Yokoi.

Gunpei Yokoi was hired by Nintendo in 1965 as a newly graduated electronics engineer. In a few years, thanks to his success with various toy and puzzle inventions, he was assigned as the general manager of Nintendo's first electronics development team. This team would later grow and, in 1978, split into two groups: Nintendo Research & Development 1 (R&D1) and Nintendo Research & Development 2 (R&D2). Yokoi remained general manager of R&D1 and was instrumental in the Game & Watch handheld line in the early 1980s and the Game Boy portable console in 1989. In addition to his considerable skills as an engineer and inventor, it is believed that Yokoi's success was also attributable to his personal design philosophy (Inoue 2010, 142; S. E. Jones and Thiruvathukal [2012]).

At the heart of Yokoi's design philosophy lay a concept he called "lateral thinking with withered technology" (Makino 2010b). Yokoi's design philosophy can be summarized as an approach that emphasized finding novel uses for existing, inexpensive technology. His philosophy arguably runs counter to conventional game industry wisdom where newer, flashier, cutting-edge technology is (assumed) better.

For example, by the early 1990s, Yokoi and Nintendo had seen significant commercial success with both the Game & Watch and Game Boy platforms. The former made use of inexpensive calculator and wristwatch LCDs and the manufacturing techniques behind them. The Game Boy utilized a similarly inexpensive monochrome dot-matrix LCD without a backlight to create a light and portable gaming device with a great battery life when compared to other contemporary handheld consoles (Custodio 2020, 36). When compared to its competitors, the inexpensive Game Boy was noticeably under-powered, yet it was significantly more successful commercially. Neither the Game & Watch nor the Game Boy were considered technologically "cutting edge" when they were released.

For Yokoi, an older technology's limitations were an opportunity— both commercially (older tech is cheaper and generally more reliable due to manufacturing experience) and creatively (reimagining its use provides opportunities for new and unexpected kinds of consumer entertainment experiences). So, how did this philosophy play out when Yokoi was presented with Reflection Technology's Private Eye display?

On the commercial side of things, the limitations inherent in the red-only display (and its potential low-power nature) caught Yokoi's imagination because it utilized inexpensive, power-sipping red LED technology. A device using this display could be manufactured and sold more cheaply and would also be more energy efficient to play: it would either use fewer batteries or play longer with the ones it had.

The Private Eye's display was creatively interesting to Yokoi because, as demonstrated by Reflection's demo, it could simulate absolute blackness in the areas where the LEDs didn't light. This provided an immersive sense of depth that Yokoi particularly enjoyed. Makino explains:

> What particularly intrigued Mr. Yokoi was the way in which the background was black. Because liquid crystal displays have a backlight, the background doesn't become black. However, Private Eye used an LED display, which meant that the non-illuminated parts became completely black.
>
> Mr. Yokoi wanted to use this "complete blackness" to allow users to experience a "limitless space." He had this thought: "how can you jump outside of the screen?" In the end, you see, games were just drawing pseudo-three-dimensional images on a screen [that simulated depth].

At some point, users were going to get tired of this, and so he wanted to create games that could really jump out of the screen. He had already made several games that interacted between the screen and the outside world, like Duck Hunt and R.O.B. (the Nintendo robot).

Mr. Yokoi had this idea that if the background was completely dark, then the screen would feel as if it stretched out in depth, indefinitely. In my interview with him as well, he talked about "extending the depth of the screen"; that was his idea, and to render it, using a 3D display was necessary. (Makino 2015)

Yokoi saw the unlimited, enveloping blackness of the Private Eye's LED-based display as an opportunity to create games without borders, hoping for a new kind of gameplay not constrained by the limitations of a TV screen. As noted earlier with regard to Japanese perceptions of VR, blocking out the outside world was a feature rather than a drawback (Roquet 2022, 7). For Yokoi, this was also a chance to broaden the audience for games. Yokoi believed that the population of people playing games was decreasing—with players less interested in having to spend a lot of money for new games that were also more difficult to play (Yokoi and Makino 2010, 168). The Virtual Boy was to be "geared toward people at the bottom of the game [pyramid]"; it was "aimed at aunts, uncles, and children" (Yokoi and Makino 2010, 168–169).

Gunpei Yokoi felt that TV-based games had reached their limits and saw stereoscopic 3D as a logical next step to take video games into a new era of design. To help secure this new era, for these new kinds of games, Nintendo obtained an exclusive license to gaming applications of the SLA and also purchased a minority stake in Reflection Technology (Nintendo of America 1995a).

Developing the Virtual Boy

At first, Yokoi intended to create a head-mounted virtual reality game console with the SLA display technology, code-named "VR32." He envisioned a third category of video games for Nintendo—beyond consoles and handhelds—called "wearables," where a player could strap the new console to their head and play on the go. The journey from "wearable" to what the Virtual Boy eventually became (a tabletop unit on a stand) largely involved worry about liability issues at Nintendo (Makino 2015)—specifically, there were concerns with the Japanese Product Liability (PL) Law that was being discussed—before ultimately going into effect in 1995 (Yokoi and Makino 2010, 169).

To balance the needs of running a CPU on battery power while also providing a modern gaming experience, the engineering team picked a relatively low-wattage 32-bit processor from NEC called the V810. NEC designed the V810 in the early 1990s for embedded applications. During this phase of development, when Yokoi still intended the console to be a wearable headset, Nintendo's engineers also developed custom chips for graphics and sound and incorporated the V810 into its own custom IC package. As fitting for an intended wearable, sound was provided via a standard headphone jack or through two speakers (on the left and right of the unit). However, liability and safety concerns would significantly alter the development trajectory of the VR32.

In the early 1990s, there was less knowledge and understanding of the potentially negative effects of electromagnetic fields (EMFs) on the brain (e.g., Glazer [1991]). These concerns would only begin to be significantly explored and addressed in the coming years as mobile/cellular telephones became increasingly popular and widely available. Since the VR32 headset prototype placed the main circuitry of the console on the wearer's head, according to Takefume Makino, there were concerns in Nintendo that they might be found liable if someone got sick from EMF exposure (Makino 2015). To address these concerns, Nintendo added metal shielding to the VR32 to block EMFs (Makino 2015). In doing so, Makino claims that the added weight from the shielding made the headset too heavy to comfortably wear on the head with a strap like a pair of goggles.

To compensate for the extra weight, Nintendo designed a special shoulder mount that allowed the player to wear the VR32 on their head while distributing weight to the neck and shoulders. Yokoi mentioned plans for making the shoulder mount available for sale commercially in a press interview with *Next Generation* magazine (*Next Generation* 1995a, 46), and Nintendo also patented it in Japan (Yokoi et al. 1997). Again, liability concerns popped up. Nintendo feared injuries from someone wearing the console while accidentally walking down the stairs or from playing it in the back seat of a car. The mental picture, and resulting PR nightmare, of someone having the VR32 smash into their face from hitting the back of a car seat during a car accident or sudden stop, was enough to warrant further changes to the device (Wells 2015). In the end, the shoulder mount was not commercially released, and it might not even have been necessary since the Virtual Boy did not, in fact, ship with any added metal shielding.

However, all these (well-placed) fears resulted in the VR32 becoming a tabletop unit on a stand. The stand solved several problems: it held the weight of the console and kept users from being mobile (a concern due to mobile injury worries). The VR32 design was thus a severe compromise that betrayed several of Yokoi's original intentions—wearability and mobility—which in turn made head tracking also unviable. The only two major design conceits that remained from the original vision were its semi-portable nature and its stereoscopic display.

Now that it was stationary, the VR32 presented something of a paradox: its chips' design had been constrained for use in a mobile device, yet it was no longer a mobile device. So, why wasn't the chipset redesigned? It seems likely that it was too late in the product development process and Nintendo was feeling pressure to release the Virtual Boy as soon as possible.

Nintendo was worried about losing market relevance (and share) by not having some kind of hardware product release. Consider that, in late 1993, the new (32-bit/64-bit) console generation had kicked off with the release of the 3DO and Atari Jaguar consoles, and 1994 would see the release of Sega's Saturn and newcomer Sony's PlayStation (Donovan 2010). Nintendo had nothing. They had been drip-feeding information about their "Ultra 64" (later renamed Nintendo 64) platform throughout the year while knowing it wouldn't be ready until 1996. So, Nintendo needed a stopgap product to please shareholders (Loguidice and Barton 2009, 258). That product was the VR32—which would soon be renamed Virtual Boy.

Yokoi had doubts about the commercial viability of the VR32 in its state at the time. Makino recounts Yokoi's feelings: "Even Mr. Yokoi admitted that he himself felt uneasy during development. He described it as a kind of 'hiri-hiri' feeling. This is an onomatopoeia that only exists in Japanese but think about it as the sort of feeling you would get when being cooked slowly over a frying pan" (Makino, as quoted in Edwards [2015]). Despite these internal doubts, Nintendo went ahead with the Virtual Boy's release.

Nintendo released the Virtual Boy first in Japan on July 21, 1995. Nintendo of America followed with a release in the United States on August 21, 1995, for $179.95, though it quickly lowered the price to $159.95 on October 18, 1995 (Nintendo of America 1995b).

Contrary to common knowledge, the Virtual Boy was also released in other countries. For example, Brazil's Playtronic—the first company in the world licensed to produce Nintendo products outside Japan (Fittipaldi 1993)—officially launched the Virtual Boy in October 1995 (*Old!Gamer* 2016, 2–50). The Brazilian release, priced at R$400' (Folhina 1995), consisted of units and games imported from the United States, with instructions in Portuguese provided via stickers on the boxes and/or inserts. The Virtual Boy was similarly available in other countries, including Canada and Mexico—though the level of additional support (e.g., manuals translated to local languages) provided by importers and/or official Nintendo distributors varied.

The End of the Virtual Boy

We have discussed the beginning of the Virtual Boy's history, its technology, how it created its stereoscopic effect, and how Virtual Boy game creators amplified this effect artistically. Any notion of a platform's history should also consider how it ended. For most platforms, their discontinuation is part of a cyclical behavior in terms of sales (Marchand and Hennig-Thurau 2013). As a platform is released, its sales climb for a few years before reaching a peak and then declining over a longer period of years. The start of the decline usually coincides with the release of a new (and usually technologically superior) platform. Thus, the discontinuation of a video game platform is often a footnote—occurring years after the platform's successor has been on the market.

This was not the case with the Virtual Boy.

After launch, public reception to the Virtual Boy proved tepid in Japan but initially promising in the United States. But the sales didn't hold up, and ultimately the console only sold 140,000 units in Japan and 630,000 in North America—for a total of 770,000 estimated units sold (Cifaldi 2011). Nintendo pulled the plug on the Virtual Boy in Japan on December 22, 1995, just six months after launch. Due to higher sales in America, Nintendo of America continued selling the Virtual Boy in that territory into 1996. In May 1996, Nintendo offered a major price cut to the Virtual Boy to $99 (Cifaldi 2011), but it wasn't enough to ignite the public's interest in the console. While internet sources sometimes claim that Nintendo discontinued the Virtual Boy in March of 1996, E3 materials from May of that year show that the system was still active with plans to release two new titles, *Bound High!* and *Dragon Hopper*, on August 26, 1996 (Nintendo of America 1996). Ultimately, neither title saw commercial release. The Virtual Boy's precise discontinuation date in America is unknown but likely occurred between May and August 1996. Either way, by late 1996 and early 1997, the Virtual Boy could regularly be found on American clearance shelves for as little as $30 (Edwards 2014).

As a dedicated game platform, the Virtual Boy was unusual in being canceled extraordinarily quickly. Even other notable game platform commercial failures had longer lifecycles (e.g., Sega's Dreamcast launched in late 1998 and was discontinued in March of 2001, and Nintendo's own Wii U platform had a little more than five years on the market). There has been speculation about why the Virtual Boy was canceled so quickly. The most credible arguments contend that two things contributed to Nintendo's decision: a lack of potential games that could turn sales around for the device and the crisis surrounding the as-yet-unreleased Nintendo 64.

Nintendo's restrictive practices in bringing third-party developers on board to develop games meant that there was a dearth of forthcoming game titles that could strengthen the platform: the release calendar was not well populated. Furthermore, the Virtual Boy's lukewarm reception meant that there were no new developers eager to sign on with new Virtual Boy titles. In other words, the Virtual Boy was not a platform for which there was either a significant number of titles in development or interest in developing new ones. The second argument explaining Nintendo's rapid cancellation was the sense of a crisis for Nintendo that was reaching a boil, with concerns that the company might even withdraw from the game market (Makino 2010a). This crisis was felt keenly by Yokoi as well, exceptionally so when Sony's PlayStation launched in 1994: "the newcomer Nintendo64 was no match for it" (Makino 2010a). By mid-1996, Nintendo was significantly behind schedule with the release of its Nintendo 64 console, and the Virtual Boy had not met sales expectations. Therefore, the company should quickly shift its resources to help the Nintendo 64. In other words, it was deemed more important (for the survival of the company) to cut losses on the Virtual Boy to increase the chances of the N64 succeeding. As Peter Main, former executive vice president of sales and marketing for Nintendo of America, noted when comparing the Virtual Boy's higher sales figures to those of the Sega Saturn—"We outsold them and we got out," and what "we learned out of it, as Sega did before us, is that working on two brand new platforms simultaneously with a finite number of creative and competent game developers is a very, very tough proposition" (Sheff and Eddy 1999, 449). Therefore, "with Virtual Boy out of the way, Nintendo didn't have any distractions to keep it from concentrating on the upcoming release of Nintendo 64" (Sheff and Eddy 1999, 450).

After a brief, interesting lifespan, the star of the Virtual Boy burned out. In August of 1996, Gunpei Yokoi resigned from Nintendo,[2] ending his long and influential run at the company. His influence on Nintendo lived on, however: the firm continued to develop products using "lateral thinking with withered technology"—the Nintendo DS and Wii are perhaps two standout examples (Tobin [2013] for the DS; S. E. Jones and Thiruvathukal [2012] for the Wii). Yokoi's philosophy is baked into Nintendo's soul.

The Virtual Boy system consists of three major components: the display assembly (in red and black), which contains the console's electronic logic, displays, speakers, and eyeshade to block out external light; a folding bipod stand that supports the unit; and the controller. The Virtual Boy's controller also serves as a power source through either six AA batteries contained in a detachable battery box or an optional AC adapter attachment that was sold separately. Virtual Boy games are stored in sixty-pin plastic molded cartridges that contain the games' software code in ROM.

To set up the Virtual Boy system for play, the display assembly must be attached to the stand using a spring-loaded clamp on the stand itself. The clamp is notoriously finicky and easy to break if forced and placed incorrectly. Also, the stand's feet should face away from the player (Nintendo 1995f, 6). Next, the battery box should be attached to the back of the controller. The battery box's cover can then be slid open, six AA batteries placed inside, and the cover slid shut. The controller's cord plug must then be inserted into the matching connector on the bottom of the display assembly. The final step, prior to sliding the power switch located on the front center face of the game controller, is to remove the protective plastic connector cover from a game cartridge and insert it into the slot on the bottom of the display unit (Nintendo 1995f).

It is an unusual setup, perhaps because the controller powers the main unit. But it is also unusual for video game play since players must lean—some would say hunch—into the device. All of this to play games in stereoscopic 3D. So, how does it actually work?

The Display

The Virtual Boy display utilizes two of Reflection Technology's SLA "scanners," one for each eye (see chapter 3). Each SLA is an array of red LEDs 224 pixels tall by one pixel wide. Each scanner "draws" an image by sweeping, from left to right, forming a 384 × 224-pixel display that has a widescreen 16:9.333 (1.71:1) display ratio (described as "wide-screen" in Nintendo 1995e).

To "sweep" the LED array, inside the display assembly for each eye, a voice coil motor rapidly oscillates a mirror left and right on a center axis fifty times per second (50 Hz). While this takes place, the LED linear array of 224 LEDs changes (switching off or on at different levels of brightness) to provide the pixels of each column in the 384 × 224 frame. Each eye perceives a two-dimensional image due to an effect known as persistence of vision: an afterimage persists (in the eye) "when a point of light moves faster than the eye can react to it" (Daukantas 2010). This is the same effect that allows us to see pictures drawn in the air in laser light shows and why we see lines on the wall when we aim a laser pointer at it and wiggle it around. In the case of the Virtual Boy, what is being "wiggled" is the LED array and what each eye perceives is a 384 × 244-pixel two-dimensional image or frame.

The Virtual Boy paints an entire 384 × 224 frame in 5 ms, during a fraction of the 20 ms frame cycle (50 Hz) where the angular velocity of the mirror is stable. Doing this properly is no simple task. If there is ever any variation in the mirror's oscillation due to gravity or motion of the unit itself, a servo control circuit reads each mirror's oscillation frequency, phase, amplitude, and offset with a reflective light beam and automatically adjusts and stabilizes the mirror to maintain the 50 Hz oscillation rate.

The Virtual Boy also has a "virtual image processor" (VIP) chip that, among other things, also does automatic "dot pitch width compensation," which dynamically adjusts the output of each LED during the mirror oscillations to make sure all the pixels appear to be the same width (Nintendo 1995e, 3-4-1). Furthermore, the Virtual Boy oscillates its right and left mirrors 180 degrees out of phase "to reduce VIP display process load and to average out the LED power consumption" (Nintendo 1995e, 3-3-1).

All of this is to say that the Virtual Boy's display was, and continues to be, unusual. Images shown on traditional television displays at the time (CRT) were "drawn" by an electron gun that fired electrons to light up phosphors on the inside of the screen. The gun (or guns, in color displays) sweeps across the screen in a horizontal line one "pixel" at a time. Once a line is complete, the gun can start sweeping the next line down, continuing thus until the entire screen has been "drawn" (at which point it resets and starts from the top again[1]) (Blundell 2008). The Virtual Boy's display instead "draws" in columns rather than rows or lines. Furthermore, it "draws" pixels in a column eight at a time from top to bottom rather than going pixel by pixel.

While the display is only capable of showing red, it is more precise to say that it displays images in four "colors" (2-bit depth per pixel), which translates to black (when showing nothing) and three shades of red. This is similar to the original Game Boy, which also supported four shades of grey: black, two shades of grey, and "white" (Nintendo 1999). In the case of the Virtual Boy, each of the three shades can additionally be picked from approximately 128 perceivable brightness levels. Therefore, even the more precise claim that the Virtual Boy displays only four shades of red is not technically correct. It turns out that the exact number of possible shades of red (i.e., the Virtual Boy's true color depth in red) is difficult to quantify because it depends on the perception of a human observer who may not be able to distinguish between slight differences in brightness.

As described here, you might think that the Virtual Boy creates a single image. However, it creates two images: one for each eye. When these two images (left and right) are slightly different from each other, in just the right way, as they are viewed together with each respective eye, players perceive a sense of depth through stereopsis.

Stereopsis is the perception of depth created by the human brain when it combines visual information from two eyes simultaneously. Specifically, "stereopsis is induced by horizontal disparity—that is, horizontal differences in the position of images" (Patterson 1992, 670). By virtue of each eye's position on the head, a human viewer will see the same scene at a slightly different angle in the left eye than in the right eye. The different apparent horizontal positions of objects in these two images (called binocular disparity) gives the human brain information about the distance of objects from the viewer, and we experience those distances as binocular depth perception.

For the Virtual Boy's stereopsis effect to be convincing and comfortable, the distance between the two SLA displays in the console housing must match the physiological distance between the eyes on the user's head. Scientists typically measure this distance as the "interpupillary distance," or IPD.

Engineers at Nintendo planned for variations in IPD between players and included an IPD dial on the top of the Virtual Boy, which allows people to customize the distance between the SLA displays. The distance between both SLA assemblies and the player's face can be changed as well using a plastic slider on the top of the display assembly labeled "Focus." As noted in the manual, failure to properly adjust the IPD dial and the focus slider "may result in headaches, nausea, dizziness, or blurred vision" (Nintendo 1995f, 13). It is possible that the Virtual Boy's notoriety for "causing headaches" was largely the result of improper configuration of the IPD, and, arguably, Nintendo could have done more to help players understand the importance of this part of the setup.

The Graphics Architecture

The Virtual Boy's architecture provides for two basic modalities for displaying images on the screen. We'll refer to them as polygon-based and tile-based. The Virtual Boy's development manual does indicate that polygon-based and tile-based approaches can coexist (Nintendo 1995e, 2-6-1), but for purposes of this chapter, we will consider them as distinct separate modalities.

The polygon-based approach mostly requires that the game developer create their own custom display engine and "write" the results directly to video RAM (VRAM). Furthermore, said programmer would have to deal with the fact that data transfers to VRAM are significantly slower than similar transfers to working RAM. Thus, the VIP does not provide any special "shortcuts" or support for polygons, and the game software has to do all the heavy lifting and drive the display directly. All of this is in a context in which speed is of the essence but direct data transfers (to VRAM) are too slow. This may be the reason why the majority of the Virtual Boy's commercially released titles were not polygon-based.

In fact, the two most notable polygon-based examples, *Red Alarm* and *3D Tetris*, were programmed by the same person—Mitsuto Nagashima from the game development company T&E Soft. In discussing the development of *Red Alarm*, he noted that "creating the graphics data was quite a challenge" and that "the level design was even more of a challenge" because the hardware "had trouble calculating all the 3D coordinates at a fast enough speed" (Nagashima in Szczepaniak [2015, 65–66]). Performance was a real challenge, and the team had to simplify aspects of its level design, reducing calculations by making levels out of "3D blocks" or lowering the precision of the math calculations (e.g., using 8 bits instead of 24 bits) when speed was more important (Szczepaniak 2015). Many of these techniques would be used in *3D Tetris* as well. Nagashima commented, when interviewed circa 2014, that he wished he "had more time to make *Red Alarm* play more smoothly and have a better framerate" (quoted in Szczepaniak [2015], 68). Regardless of the game's limitations, it impressed Nintendo enough that they decided to show it at the E3 expo in Los Angeles, where it was compared favorably with *Star Fox*.

So, although we stated earlier that the Virtual Boy provides for two modalities in terms of graphics support, it is more fair to say that it could display 3D polygonal graphics in the same way that any computational platform can handle polygons, including, for example, the Atari 2600 (e.g., Kylearan [2014, 2, 57]). So, it's a "modality" by default rather than by explicit support. As a modality, it might be more accurate to describe it as "Do whatever you want; the hardware won't make things easier."

In practice, the Virtual Boy hardware's design and strengths lay in supporting the tile-based approach. This modality is, by far, better documented and supported in Nintendo's *Virtual Boy Development Manual* (Nintendo 1995e). The tile-based approach, common to other game consoles of the time (e.g., the SNES, as detailed in Arsenault [2017]), consists of a collection of data abstractions and hardware configuration (e.g., the VIP processor, predesignated areas of RAM memory, and so on) that allow for the efficient processing of 2D graphics data.

The first abstraction is the tile ("character" in the official documentation). A tile is an image that is 8×8 pixels. Each pixel is represented internally using 2 bits (thus allowing for each pixel to be one of four colors including "transparent," but more on this later). The Virtual Boy's memory allocates space for storing up to 2,048 tiles subdivided into four blocks, each with 512 tiles (Nintendo 1995e, 5-6-1, 5-7-1). The tile is the basic building block from which everything shown on the displays is created.

The next abstraction is a background map (BG map). A BG map is a mosaic of 64×64 tiles. Note that at 512×512 pixels, the BG map is larger than the screen's display. The Virtual Boy assigns enough RAM memory to store up to fourteen BG maps, and these can be combined in ten specific configurations to create even larger maps as you might see in a long-scrolling 2D platformer (Nintendo 1995e, 5-11-1).

The third major data abstraction are objects (OBJs). Objects are generally used for display elements that will move around on the screen (e.g., enemies as opposed to static background elements), and the Virtual Boy assigns enough memory for 1,024 objects. An object consists of a tile with some additional attributes including a screen coordinate, a parallax offset (more on this later), which display it should appear on (left and/or right), and what color palette to use. When developers want to display a moving element that is larger than a single tile (8×8 pixels), it would have to be created using more than one object. Colloquially, OBJs can be considered a form of sprite.

The last major data abstraction is called a *world*. These are referred to as "layers of virtual surface" (Nintendo 1995e, 5-1-1), and there are thirty-two of them. We can think of a VB world as a transparent "window" on which "stickers" (images) can be placed. In this analogy, there are two types of stickers—the aforementioned backgrounds and objects. Therefore, to create a scene in a game, a programmer would organize the data for different backgrounds and objects by indicating on which world they are as well as their position in that world. In terms of limitations, "either one [background] or up to 1024 [objects] (distributed through up to 4 worlds) can be placed in each world" (Nintendo 1995e, 5-1-1).

To prepare an image for display, the VIP chip examines and processes the content of each world starting with World 31. The idea is that World 31 is the one furthest away from the player, while World 0 is the one on the front. By processing the worlds in this order, the information in the lower-numbered worlds can "overwrite" that in the higher-numbered ones. Going back to our transparent window metaphor, if you place each window on top of another, the stickers (backgrounds or objects) on the window on the world closest to the front (World 0) occlude the stickers on the other worlds when they are in the same position. However, the different world numbers do not indicate depth in the depth perception/stereoscopy sense. We discuss more on how depth is handled in the next section.

As a final step in this simplified explanation for how the Virtual Boy displays images, the Virtual Boy uses a double framebuffer for each display. Generally speaking, a framebuffer is an area of memory where the content that will be shown on the display is stored. In a double-buffered system, one frame has the information for the current image to be shown on screen. While that information is being displayed, the information for the next image is being copied over to the second framebuffer. Once this process is completed, the second framebuffer becomes the current one, and then new data is copied into what was previously the active framebuffer. In this way, the next image to be shown is being prepared while the current one is being displayed, and the framebuffers alternate between being shown/displayed and being prepared for display.

Since the Virtual Boy has two displays, it has a total of four framebuffers. The Virtual Boy's displays are "drawn" in a specific order—first the left display and then the right one. As mentioned earlier, each display alternates getting data from each of its frame buffers. We note that, although the displays "draw" in columns as mentioned earlier, the frame buffers' data is "filled" in row-major order (that is, each row is filled from left to right starting with the top row and continuing down to the bottom row).

How the Virtual Boy handles color is slightly more complicated. Since LEDs are only "on" or "off," the apparent brightness is changed by pulsing how long each LED is lit. The longer the pulse, the brighter the apparent shade of red. As noted earlier, the Virtual Boy officially supports 2-bit color, with four values per palette, three red and one black or transparent. The VIP supports four palettes for OBJs, four for BGs, and one for background color settings (Nintendo 1995e, 5-12-1), including support for a "transparent" color. Going back to our "sticker" analogy, when a sticker's pixel is assigned the "transparent" color, it acts as a "hole" that does not occlude what is behind. It is also technically possible, by directly altering the brightness registers at opportune moments, to show more than three shades of red on-screen at a time. The intro scene of *Virtual Boy Wario Land* does this by fading certain parts of the image (Perfect 2014).

Each palette of four color values is chosen by the game developer and pulled from 256 different theoretical levels of brightness (each of the three brightness registers has 8 bits, and thus 256 different possible values). The value of the registers corresponds to how long the LED will remain on, but practical experience indicates that values above 127 do not result in increased brightness (Perfect 2014). The exact number of visible color shades possible on the Virtual Boy is thus difficult to pin down because of how the eye perceives the light, which can also vary from individual to individual. The VIP color palette also has other limitations. The brightest color cannot be darker than the other two values since its brightness value is the sum of all three color registers (CLKA+CLKB+CLKC) (Nintendo 1995e, 5-23-1).

Creating the 3D Stereoscopic Effect

Artists have used and developed a variety of techniques to create the illusion of depth. For example, the use of perspective, shading, and scaling objects. In addition to these techniques (and others), animators learned to move background layers at different speeds (relative to each other), giving an illusion of depth called "parallax effect" when layers closer to the eye moved much faster than those further away (see chapter 5 for a more detailed discussion). All of these techniques were well known and widely used at the time in video games prior to the Virtual Boy's release. For example, Nintendo's Super NES supported two to four background layers (in Mode 0) and made wide use of the parallax effect by scrolling these backgrounds at different speeds (Arsenault 2017).

All of this to say that, while the Virtual Boy's hardware's key graphical feature was its capability of generating a stereoscopic view, its game creators also made use of the other artistic and technical methods known and used in video games at the time.

The Virtual Boy achieves stereopsis by generating two images containing slight differences. The differences lie in the horizontal position of the same object in each image. Depending on the direction and size (in pixels) of that horizontal difference in position of the object in each image, an object appears closer (or further) to the player when compared to an object in the same position in both displays. Figure 4.1 shows three versions of the same image, one for each eye and the third representing the "reconstruction"—that is, what the viewer perceives. Each image has three objects: triangle, circle, and oval. The circle shape is in exactly the same position (there is no horizontal displacement) in all the images. The triangle, however, is shifted inward—toward the right for the left eye image and toward the left for the right eye image. In other words, the triangle is shifted toward the viewer's nose in the image for each eye and will appear closer to the viewer (relative to the other shapes). The oval, on the other hand, is shifted outward—toward the left for the left eye image and toward the right for the right eye image. Here, the shift in the images for both eyes is away from the viewer's nose, and the oval will appear further from the viewer (relative to the other shapes). The circle will appear to be between the other two shapes: further away from the triangle and closer than the oval.

Again, we note that the effect of perceived depth is relative and based on the context of objects around it. During experiments prior to the creation of *Red Alarm*, developer Mitsuto Nagashima found that if he placed a single

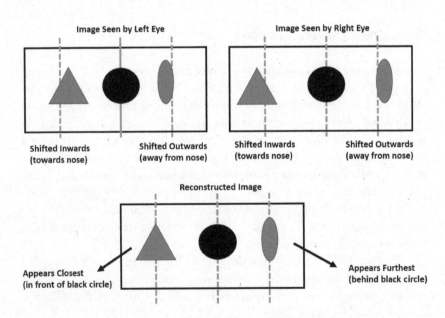

4.1 Stereoscopy achieved via horizontal displacement (based on image in Nintendo [1995e, 2-4-1]).

object on the Virtual Boy screen with parallax (horizontal) displacement against a black background, he could not perceive the depth of the object (Szczepaniak 2015). In other words, if only one of the shapes in figure 4.1 was displayed, a viewer would not be able to determine how far or close it was.

The object that is in the same location in both images (for left and right eye), the circle in figure 4.1, is in a position in which the eyes do not detect any disparity. This point—technically a fixed distance from the eyes—is called the horopter. The horopter is sort of a baseline for the brain against which whatever the eyes are seeing is compared. Figure 4.2 below shows a top-down view of two eyes fixating on a point F. Here, point F is on the horopter, the same as point A. Point A is seen by each eye in points a and a' for the left and right eye, respectively. Since the angle between a and f (left eye) and a' and f' (right eye) is the same—there is no disparity (note that the image is not drawn to scale). This is not the same for object B however, which is seen at points b and b'. Notice that the distance between f and b and f' and b' are not the same. Because of this disparity and because the angle $f'b'$ in the right eye is larger than the angle fb in the left eye—object B will be perceived as being closer. It is the opposite for objects behind the horopter. Also, objects that are at a greater distance from the horopter (in front or behind) will have a greater disparity than those closer. The Virtual Boy was designed such that when the same image was shown on both displays (no disparity), it would "appear to be at a distance of approximately 1 meter from the player" and "its size [would appear] to be approximately 18 inches" (Nintendo 1995e, A-1). Nintendo referred to this as the "Virtual Screen" and informed developers that players looking at images on the Virtual Screen (no horizontal disparity) would be the least straining to players' eyes (Nintendo 1995e, A-2). We can think of the "Virtual Screen" as the horopter.

Images positioned closer than the horopter (the neutral point) are said to have "crossed disparities," and objects farther than the horopter have "uncrossed disparities" (Patterson 1992). Understanding this is important to understanding the Virtual Boy's limitations in terms of perceived depth.

So, how did game developers create stereoscopic imagery? That is, given a graphical element, how did they determine how deep or close it should appear in relation to the "Virtual Screen"? This is where the VIP comes in. When Virtual Boy game developers position graphical elements on the screen, they specify the traditional X and Y coordinates and also a parallax attribute used to indicate depth. The parallax attribute specifies the amount graphical elements should be shifted from their centers in the left and right displays to create the parallax depth effect. The VIP handles the arithmetic (e.g., additions/subtractions to the X coordinate) automatically.

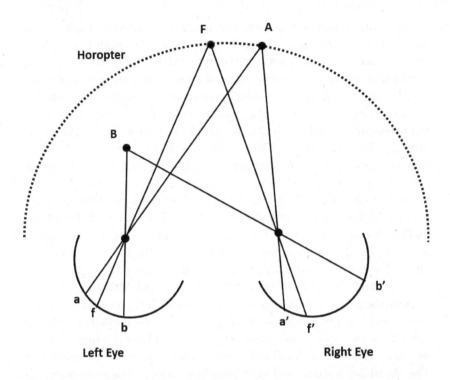

4.2 A top-down view of eyes looking at objects (adapted from image in Patterson [1992]).

However, the game developer must determine what depth they want graphical elements to appear at: in front or behind the Virtual Screen, and by how much.

So, how much variation in depth is possible? Well, it depends. For OBJs, the parallax attribute is a 14-bit signed integer with 16,383 possible values: from −8,191 to 8,191 (Nintendo 1995e, 5-8-1). Since this value is measured in pixels and is subtracted for elements to be shown to the left eye and added for those intended for the right eye, this means that there are technically 8,191 depths in front of the Virtual Screen and the same number behind.[2] In practice, the possible number of depths is dramatically smaller. This is because there is a limitation in the width of the Virtual Boy's display area (384 pixels). Additionally, there are limits to the human brain's ability to comfortably turn the difference between two images (the horizontal disparity) into a stereoscopic image. Nintendo created general guidelines for comfortable disparity values in Virtual Boy game development (Nintendo 1995e, A-5): They settled on a maximum uncrossed disparity of fifty-six pixels or less, and a maximum crossed disparity of three hundred pixels for one OBJ. Nintendo also suggested a "comfort zone" for reduced eye strain and comfort: an uncrossed disparity of thirty pixels or less, a crossed disparity of forty-two pixels or less, and a relative disparity of forty pixels or less.

Ultimately, however, it was up to developers to experiment with different values to determine what worked best for their games. It is also worth noting that it is technically possible to display a completely different image on each screen. However, this would obviously create discomfort and break the stereoscopic illusion, so Nintendo warned its developers not to do so (Nintendo 1995e, A-6).

Other Tricks

In addition to being able to (relatively) quickly prepare two sets of graphical data for each display, the Virtual Boy's Visual Image Processor chip had a few additional tricks up its sleeve. To explain these, we need to briefly discuss the SNES and its famous graphics Mode 7. This mode allowed for a background image to be rotated, scaled, and more. It was also used to "generate pseudo–3-D experiences through an impressive perspective effect" (Arsenault 2017, 121).

Mode 7 perspective effects were impressive at the time, and Nintendo used them in famous games like *Pilotwings* and *Super Mario Kart*. However, the effect was fragile and required additional technical effort to maintain. For instance, because the scaling was not applicable to sprites (only to a single background), it was necessary to include multiple copies of the game's sprites in different sizes—and then display the correct sprite at the right moment such that sprites "further away" were smaller in size than those closer to the player (Arsenault 2017).

The Virtual Boy also had a similar "mode" that allowed for a background to be scaled (enlarged or reduced) and rotated. Additionally, the Virtual Boy's VIP adjusted for parallax (technically this "mode" is an attribute of a world in addition to an Affine table that stores additional parameters). Unlike the SNES Mode 7, the Virtual Boy was not limited to a single background, and this mode could be applied to multiple graphical elements. This suggests that the VIP represented an improvement over SNES's Mode 7. However, the VIP simply was not fast enough to make impressive use of these capabilities—especially when considering it had to generate two displays' worth of data. So, it is fair to say that the Virtual Boy's equivalent to the SNES Mode 7 was comparatively worse and also rarely implemented in games outside of flashy non-gameplay sequences. Nintendo's *Mario's Tennis* is a notable example of this mode in practice, as it was used to render the tennis court and scale the characters as they moved around (see figure 4.3).

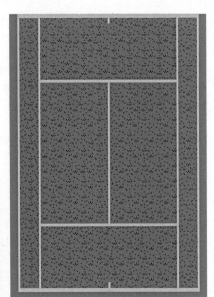

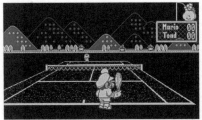

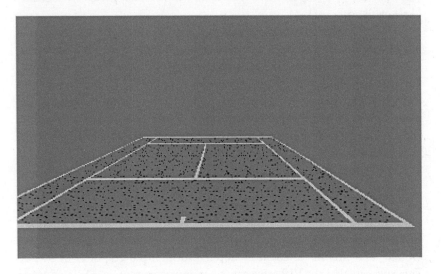

4.3 A portion of a BG for the tennis court (top left), the same tennis court in an affine world (top right), and the final display (left eye only).

Creating the Stereoscopic Effect—Artistically

For centuries, artists have provided a sensation of depth via a variety of techniques, including shading and perspective. This applies to Virtual Boy art as well. Consider figure 4.4. Imagine that this figure represents a flat-topped pyramid as viewed from above. The top of this pyramid has a "frowny face" in the center, and there are diagonal lines headed to the corners of the image from the corners of the pyramid's top.

While there is some sense of depth in figure 4.4, it could be improved with the addition of some shading. Figure 4.5 is the same flat-topped pyramid as viewed from above, but now the top and left sides of the pyramid are lighter in color, as if a source of light is hitting the top-left corner of

4.4   A flat-topped pyramid seen from above.

4.5 A flat-topped pyramid seen from above, with shading.

the pyramid. Notice also how figure 4.4 could also easily be interpreted as a "frowny face" at the bottom of a cube-shaped hole. The shading added to figure 4.5 makes this interpretation harder to sustain—strengthening and stabilizing the intended perception of depth, that is, that the "frowny face" is closer to the viewer.

If we were to view this image in a Virtual Boy (the same image in the same location on the display in both eyes), the sense of depth would be no different than what you may see on the page right now. There would be no stereoscopic effect.

As described, the Virtual Boy creates its stereoscopic effect by displacing graphical elements horizontally in relation to elements on the Virtual Screen. This is the basic functionality offered by the platform and allows for the simplest type of stereoscopic effect as illustrated in figure 4.1 earlier.

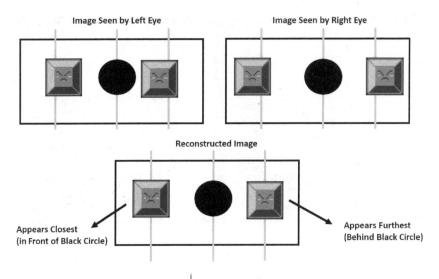

4.6 Stereoscopy achieved via horizontal displacement (see also figure 4.1).

In figure 4.6, we show how this would be done with our flat-top pyramid. Again, the circle in the center of each image is in the same position for both eyes and the left pyramid has a crossed horizontal disparity, while the pyramid on the right as an uncrossed horizontal disparity.

The technique shown in figure 4.6 is simple and is enhanced artistically due to the shading on the flat-topped pyramids when compared to figure 4.1. In terms of "using stereo," these kinds of images are the easiest (and arguably least sophisticated) to create.

So, Virtual Boy game developers used additional techniques for more sophisticated tile-based stereoscopic images. The three most common techniques are:

1. flat element stereo ("billboards," as seen in figure 4.6)

2. stereo-within graphical element

3. aggregate-element stereo.

The stereo-within graphical element technique, simply put, is to create two versions of the same graphical element: one for each eye. The differences between these two versions create their own stereo effect, even when both elements are shown in the same position in both displays. The benefit of this technique is that it allows for a better stereoscopic effect, while the drawback is additional work in terms of creating the graphical elements, and the elements also take up more storage space on the game cartridge.

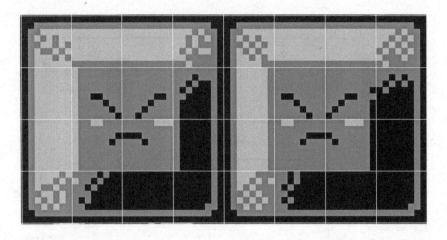

4.7 The *Virtual Boy Wario Land* frowny-face block: left-eye version and right-eye version.

We can see how this technique was used in *Virtual Boy Wario Land*. *Virtual Boy Wario Land* is a side-scrolling platforming game in which Wario can jump on top of blocks (as well as breaking them when hitting them from below). Figure 4.7 shows one of the blocks used in the game. The game includes two versions of the same block with slight differences between them. The block on the left is intended for the left eye, while the other would only be shown to the right.

In the center of each block, with a slightly darker color, we can see a depiction of a frowny face (the same as our "flat-topped pyramid" used earlier—it was a block all along!). The white grid lines have been added separately and are placed exactly eight pixels apart, illustrating how the block is composed of sixteen tiles. The white lines also help visualize where the middle of the block is in terms of its pixel width and height. Note how, unlike figures 4.4 and figure 4.5, the frowny face in the center of the block is not symmetrically arranged with regards to the vertical axis of symmetry. Furthermore, the asymmetry of the face within the block is different between the left-eye block and the right-eye one. On the left block, the frowny face is shifted right of center: the left eyebrow touches the white vertical gridline that is the vertical axis of symmetry. If the face was centered, it would appear shifted exactly one pixel to the left, and the left eyebrow would not touch the vertical white gridline. The right block's frowny face is shifted left-of-center (the opposite of the left block): notice that the right eyebrow touches the white vertical gridline.

The horizontal disparities of the frowny faces (eyebrows, cheeks, and mouth), with respect to the block's external edges are crossed—thus, when

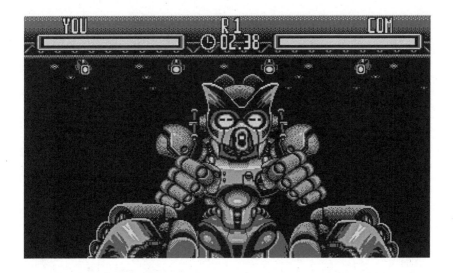

4.8 A screenshot from *Teleroboxer*.

viewed in the Virtual Boy, the frowny face appears to be in front of the rest of the block. In this way, by creating two different versions of the same graphical element and showing one to each eye, a stereoscopic effect can be achieved even when the graphical element is in the same position in each of the Virtual Boy's displays. Of course, this could be placed with a horizontal disparity—thus appearing in front or behind of other elements. For this technique Nintendo recommended not having more than four to five pixels of horizontal disparity within the same element so as to not cause discomfort (Nintendo 1995e, A-6).

The third technique, aggregate-element stereo, is when different graphical elements are positioned in relation to each other to form a larger figure, and those elements are themselves positioned with certain disparities. At the time of Virtual Boy's release, it was relatively common for some games to feature large enemy "bosses" that were made up of multiple sprites that were animated separately. This technique is essentially a variation of that—but with forethought into achieving an interesting stereoscopic view.

Figure 4.8 is a screenshot from *Teleroboxer*, a first-person boxing game where the player (depicted only by two robotic fists at the bottom of the screen) must fight other robots.

The enemy robot the player fights against is an example of the aggregate-element stereo technique. The robot is made up of eleven different graphical elements (and two additional "masking" elements): head, shoulder ball (left and right), fists (left and right), chest, stomach/mid-riff, hip coils

4.9 Some of the graphical elements that make up an enemy boxer in *Teleroboxer*.

(one element for left and right sides), groin, and thighs (left and right). These elements are animated independently of each other and, for a richer stereoscopic effect, also placed at different horizontal disparities (e.g., the robot's fists are the closest to the viewer). These disparities can be changed. For example, while the shoulder balls are usually at the same level of depth, when the robot's left fist moves toward the camera, the corresponding shoulder ball can also move forward while the other shoulder ball does not.

The aggregate-element stereo technique was also used in more nuanced and subtle ways than a large on-screen character (as in *Teleroboxer*, described earlier). For example, a technical write-up examining *Virtual Boy Wario Land* describes how even simple enemy characters that might seem to be implemented via simple graphical objects are, in fact, composed by layering and overlapping a variety of small graphical objects—often one for each moving part of the enemy (e.g., arms, legs, and eyes) such that you can achieve "a sense of depth to the character by slightly adjusting the horizontal offsets of each part depending on which eye they are being viewed from" while also allowing different body parts to be animated separately (Pizza Rolls Royce 2023). In the case of *Virtual Boy Wario Land*, the titular protagonist is made up of thirty-two overlapping 8×8-pixel objects, and "each part of Wario (arms, legs, feet, and so on) are animated independently and offset horizontally depending on which viewpoint (left or right) is being rendered to give that sense of depth" (Pizza Rolls Royce 2023). Even Wario's eye is special—it has its own set of animation frames that "shows him looking around and blinking irrespective of what the rest of his body is doing" (Pizza Rolls Royce 2023).

What we've described as three different techniques are not mutually exclusive. Virtual Boy game creators often mixed and combined these, even within the same scene. The *Teleroboxer* screenshot has all three, in fact! The life-bars and timer are one "billboard," and there are two more "billboards" that make up the background. The enemy robot, as mentioned, is created using the aggregate-element technique, but there are two different sprite versions of its head (one for each eye) that make use of the stereo-within graphical element technique.

To be clear, we are not arguing that these are the only ways that Virtual Boy's game developers created stereographic imagery artistically. These are coarse, yet distinct, categories presented to give a general sense of the variety of stereoscopic imagery seen in the games. Developers used other combinations of techniques, such as combining polygons and tile-based graphics, as well.

In the next chapter, we will show how the Virtual Boy's graphical affordances supported the platform's distinctive visual signature: the layered diorama.

In their book *Racing the Beam*, Montfort and Bogost (2009) argue that the Atari 2600's games had a shared visual aesthetic, or visual signature (Therrien and Picard 2016), that resulted, partly, from the way the platform was architected to interface with television sets of the era. Its technical design (and constraints) delineated what it could display and how it displayed them. Over the years, programmers continued exploring the hardware, discovering new tricks to achieve novel visual effects that further strengthened the "Atari 2600 style."

Having a visual signature does not make the Atari 2600 unique. All game platforms have specific graphical affordances such as a certain screen resolution, limited color palettes, restrictions on how many colors can be shown, and more. The game platform's hardware architecture also matters—by specifying how many objects can move on screen, how the platform's memory is organized and accessed, how many graphical objects can be stored, or how graphics should be encoded (Does it use tiles? What color palette should it use?)—just to name a few examples.

Each game platform's visual signature is less distinct today than it was in the 1970s and 1980s, right up until the mid-2000s. While different modern game consoles (platforms) still retain their visual signature, the differences are now subtle and are more often related to the affordances of the tools (e.g., game engines) used during the game development process than the particular hardware of the platform in question. Today, the concept of a platform's visual signature exists mostly as a form of video game nostalgia where new (often indie) games are created to visually recall the "look" of games on earlier hardware (e.g., Juul [2019]). These include low-resolution MSX computer pixel style graphics (Camper 2009), low-polygon PlayStation-era graphics, early personal computer four-color CGA graphics (Sloan 2016), Flash-style vector graphics (Salter and Murray 2014), and more.

In this chapter, we will explain how the Virtual Boy—thanks to its unique stereoscopic displays and hardware architecture—has a visual signature that goes beyond its red graphics. We call the Virtual Boy's signature aesthetic the *layered diorama*. It is an aesthetic used, in varying degrees, in many of the Virtual Boy's commercially published games. The layered diorama style has gone largely unappreciated and unrecognized.[1] This is because it cannot easily be discerned from simple examination of screenshots or non-stereoscopic play (e.g., via emulation) of the Virtual Boy's games: the style really takes playing on the original hardware to appreciate.

The layered diorama aesthetic is one where the player experiences (looks at and plays in) a miniature boxed game environment (the diorama) whose elements, rather than being fully three-dimensional, are instead flat (two-dimensional). The flat elements are placed at different distances from the viewer, thus constituting the layers of the layered diorama (see figure 5.1).

As an aesthetic, it only really "works" when the viewer/player can distinguish that there is distance (depth) between the flat elements in the diorama (gameworld). We note that to experience this aesthetic (in video game form) requires the illusion of depth perception (stereoscopy), which the Virtual Boy achieves via its stereoscopic display.

The layered diorama, as a video game aesthetic, is very much of its time (the mid-1990s). By this we mean that it is the "obvious" answer to the following question: What do you get when you have a team of game creators with significant expertise in designing sprite/tile-based graphics who need to showcase a device's stereoscopic displays but don't have enough computing power to provide real-time 3D rendered polygonal graphics that can compete with those seen in some arcade and computer games at the time?

The 1990s were a transitionary decade in terms of the graphical capabilities and visual expectations surrounding video games (see chapters 2 and 6), namely the transition from 2D sprite or tile-based graphics to 3D polygonal ones (Arsenault et al. 2013; Järvinen 2002). While the Virtual Boy's hardware was capable of handling both polygonal and tile-based graphics, its strengths were definitely for the latter rather than the former (see chapter 4). As graphics technologies improved, the constraints that made the layered diorama an aesthetic of choice for a stereoscopic system have largely been resolved: There is no longer a need to use sprites/tiles over polygonal graphics due to lack of processing power or memory limitations. This explains why the layered diorama style is largely absent in

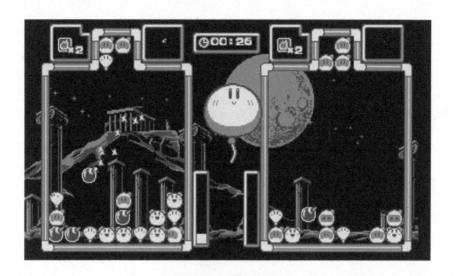

5.1 A screenshot of *Panic Bomber* (above) and a simplified recreation of its layers (below). Image by Carter Johnson (below).

games on later stereoscopic platforms like Nintendo's 3DS platform (2011) or the variety of systems released since the Oculus Rift revived popular interest in virtual reality in 2012. As Arsenault (2017, 106) notes, it does not matter how many flat 2D planes you layer—you will never achieve the 3D cinematic space that polygons can provide. When you can easily fully render 3D polygonal objects and view them stereoscopically, why bother with flat objects?

We will now show how the Virtual Boy's *layered diorama* visual signature draws from, and exists alongside, representational traditions in other media like peepshow devices, animated film, and theater. We will conclude by describing some of the different forms this style takes in the context of the Virtual Boy's softography.

The Layered Diorama

In chapter 2, we discussed the early tradition of peep boxes: devices we peer into through small viewports to view miniature worlds. Over the centuries that these devices were developed and popularized, they used a variety of techniques and technologies to provide amusement for those who paid to view their wonders.

These techniques included the use of mirrors, lenses, lights, and carefully crafted illustrations made using vanishing points and perspective. One technique, perhaps the simplest, was to use a series of images that were cut out and placed in succession from front to back—with those closest to the viewer partially obscuring those behind. Here, there was a real (non-illusionary) perception of depth that was augmented through the careful design of the images themselves, scaling and distancing them from each other such as to create the illusion of greater depth than what the dimensions of the peep box provided (see figure 5.2).

Of course, this technique of using flat layered images was not invented for peep boxes: it builds on techniques used in theater and puppetry. In theater, scenery is often painted on flat surfaces ("flats") that are then placed at different depths on the stage. A simple setup might consist of a background "flat" (e.g., depicting sky or faraway mountains) and a pair of "wing flats" situated closer to the audience on both sides of the stage (e.g., depicting bushes or rocks). The actors could enter the stage in front of the background but from behind the wing flats. A more sophisticated scenographic design could include more layers (flats) with cutouts that actors could walk through or around (e.g., a forest made up of side-by-side trees with space between them to walk through). These techniques have also been used in puppetry, including shadow puppetry.

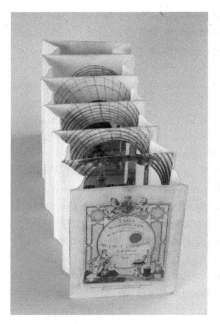 

5.2 An accordion-style paper peepshow (left) of the inside of Crystal Palace for the grand opening by Queen Victoria (right, as seen through peephole). Photos by Special Collections at Johns Hopkins University (2006), Creative Commons BA.[2]

The Virtual Boy's layered diorama style is no different. Arguably, the Virtual Boy is effectively a digital peep box that, due to its strengths in displaying flat sprites and tiles (versus polygonal graphics), provides a viewing experience similar to the simpler peep boxes of the seventeenth century. Of course, the Virtual Boy extends the medium of the peep box by allowing for both sophisticated motion and interactivity.

Another strand of influence for the Virtual Boy's layered diorama aesthetic comes from traditional animated movies. Animated film creators have also struggled with the challenge of creating flat images that, when animated, provide an illusion of depth when viewed on the screen. Over the years, they developed novel techniques (in addition to those used in traditional drawing, such as vanishing point perspective) to address this challenge.

For example, it is common in cartoon animation, especially of the hand-drawn variety, to use different images that are then layered to create a frame of animation. This technique was developed in the early twentieth century (Barrier 1999). Its simplest expression consists of only two layers: a character painted on a transparent sheet of celluloid, which is then laid on top of a separate sheet depicting only a painted background. This technique allowed for cheaper production costs since there was no need to paint the background again for the next frame of animation. The animator could simply replace the character "cel" with a new one using the same painted background from the last frame.

In 1915, animator William C. Nolan "came up with the idea of making wider background drawings and then moving them under the camera, a little in one direction or the other, each time a frame of film was exposed. Such movement encouraged the illusion that the camera was moving on a track parallel to moving characters. Animators very quickly realized that they could combine celluloid overlays of foreground elements with Nolan's innovation: foreground shrubbery that moved on and off the screen more rapidly than the background drawing, as if it were closer to the camera, enhanced the illusion of depth" (Barrier 1999, 15–16).

However, this illusion of depth was slight, and the desire to create more realistic animation led to further technical improvements. Perhaps the most famous of these was Disney's multiplane camera—"an apparatus used to create three-dimensionality within an animated image" (Pallant 2011, 27). In scenes shot using the multiplane camera, "the animation, background paintings, and overlay paintings might be on as many as six different levels, with the backgrounds and overlays painted on sheets of glass mounted a foot or more apart. As the camera trucked forward, different levels would come in and out of focus, as if they had been photographed by a live-action camera" (Barrier 1999, 249). Additionally, to further augment the illusion of depth, different layers could be moved relative to each other at different speeds: that is, the background elements are animated to move past the camera more slowly than elements in the foreground.

The technique of having different graphical layers and moving them at different speeds relative to each other is also commonly used in 2D computer graphics. It was popularized by early arcade games like *Moon Patrol* but became more widely used in the 16-bit console era (in *Super Mario World*, for example) when rendering multiple independent layers of graphics became more practical (Arsenault 2017, 106). In games that used this technique, "the closer [layers] of graphics are to the forefront, the faster they move laterally during scrolling. [Layers] farther back [. . .] scroll more slowly than those in front of them, producing a parallax effect" (Wolf 2009, 157). This technique was commonly called "parallax scrolling."

Of course, all of these technical effects are augmented by careful artistic direction—by "painting" the game's elements so they appear to have depth, for example. Game artists could also use different kinds of perspective (lines converging to a single "vanishing point" as they "move" away from the viewer) or parallel projections of different kinds (often incorrectly

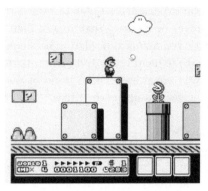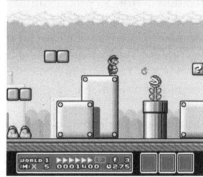

5.3 Cosmetic differences used to provide illusion of depth. Image from Arsenault and Larochelle (2013).

referred together as "isometric") where "all three axes (X, Y and Z) and thus dimensions of the represented objects are made visible from a single viewpoint" (Arsenault and Larochelle 2013, 6).

Other techniques might include shading objects in a certain way. Figure 5.3 compares screenshots from *Super Mario Bros. 3* (1988) and the same game as it appeared in the compilation title *Super Mario All-Stars* (1993)—the gameplay was unchanged but the graphics were updated providing more detail—note the addition of differences in the background, the rectangular blocks Mario is standing on, and the vertical colored lines on the green "pipes." In the case of the pipes, it's the vertical colored lines that give the illusion that the object has volume, and thus looks like a round pipe rather than two green rectangles.

Of course, there is an important difference between the theater flats and dioramas with flat layers and the techniques used in animated movies and the parallax scrolling popularized in games. In theater and dioramas, the viewer is presented with a scene in which there is actually depth. The eye is not tricked into perceiving a foreground element as being closer—it really is! If there is any illusion involved, it is in how the different elements are painted (artistically rendered) and how their relation to each other provides an illusion of greater depth than what there actually is. For example, a theater's flats might be painted such that it looks like the stage goes further back. In contrast, animated movies and parallax scrolling in video games only present an illusion—the viewer is not looking at objects placed at different physical distances from each other.

This puts the Virtual Boy's layered diorama aesthetic in an interesting place: it is an illusion (stereoscopy) built on another illusion (parallax scrolling) trying to provide an aesthetic experience similar to one that has actual depth (flat layers in peep boxes or theater) that are, in turn, augmented by an illusion (careful artistic rendering and relation between flat layers). The Virtual Boy combines these techniques and elements to provide an aesthetic experience that was novel even when none of the techniques or elements were, by themselves, unique at the time.

Distinct Variations of the Layered Diorama Style

The layered diorama style is used in all of the Virtual Boy's commercially released games. However, it is not used all the time, nor in the same way across different games. In some games, it is used only in the title screen, interstitials, or game menus, while in others it is used during gameplay. Rather than catalog how this style appears in all of the Virtual Boy's softography, we will map out the main ways the style is used. Some key distinctions we draw are:

- Does the layered diorama style appear during moments of gameplay (or not)?
- Does the game's gameplay make use of or participate in the different layers (or not)? (And if so, in what ways?)
- What is the camera perspective?

The first distinction simply acknowledges that, in some games, the layered diorama style is not used during moments of active gameplay—but rather when players are selecting options from the menus, watching interstitial animations, or viewing the title screen. As such, these games are weak examples of the layered diorama style.

With those games set aside, we now consider those games in which the layered diorama style appears during moments of gameplay. Here we can now examine whether or not the layered diorama style is relevant to the game's action or gameplay and how.

In *Mario's Tennis*, the player is presented with a third-person view of a tennis court with the controllable character at the bottom of the screen. The tennis court is angled away from the player, and the player can move the character freely (left to right and also close/far from the camera) around their side of the court in order to hit, smash, or lob the ball.[3] The layered diorama aspects are not used in the tennis court but rather in the backgrounds (far) behind the court—these depend on the match being played. In the screenshots in figure 5.4, there are hills in the background

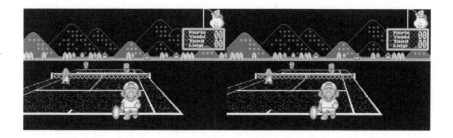

5.4 A screenshot of *Mario's Tennis* (both left and right eye).

as well as trees and houses. The background is a single graphical element. However, it has been created using the stereo-within technique described in chapter 4. The resulting effect is that there are discernable layers that make up the background area of the game with, for example, the trees noticeable in front of the hills (see the screenshot in figure 5.4).

In the case of *Mario's Tennis*, the layered diorama style is present during moments of gameplay, but it is not significant to gameplay in any way. In fact, Mario (in the screenshot) can freely move away/toward the fixed camera. Thus, Mario's movement is not restricted to (distinguishable) layers—rather, it is continuous.

Golf is another example where the layered diorama style is present during gameplay, but it plays a more important role than in *Mario's Tennis*. The game's main view presents a first-person view of a golf course that is quite crude by today's standards, with a heads-up display (HUD) interface along the top that makes use of several different layers (at least six that are easily distinguishable). The various elements provide information for the player such as the current wind speed and direction, a bird's eye view of the hole, a radar showing the direction the player is facing for the shot, and a few more elements.

In *Golf* (T&E Soft 1995a), the player can select between four rectangular icons located in the center of the HUD (almost in the middle of the screen). The currently selected icon is closest to the player, and when the player selects the icons to the left or right, they shift (rotate) such that they occupy the center space. These icons are the primary way to play the game since they are used to determine the direction of the shot, which club to use, and the power to be used in the shot (T&E Soft 1995b, 16). Not all of the game's gameplay occurs in this interface system, but *Golf* is an interesting example where the HUD is central to playing the game since it is an interface that is manipulated by the player to make (most) of their gameplay decisions. As such, *Golf* is sort of a halfway point between *Mario's Tennis* and our next example, *Panic Bomber*.

Panic Bomber (Hudson Soft 1995a) (released in Japan as *Tobidase! Panibon*, Hudson Soft 1995c) is a competitive "falling blocks" puzzle game where the player competes against a series of increasingly challenging AI opponents. Here the blocks are objects of varying shapes, each composed of three pieces. As with most games of this genre, the player must rotate and/or move them side to side. "Once three of the same blocks are in a row vertically, horizontally or diagonally they disappear and an equivalent number of unlit bombs appear at the bottom of [the player's] screen" (Hudson Soft 1995b, 12).

Players can then cause the unlit bombs to explode via lit bombs that drop in from the top, which results in "scorched bombs" appearing in the opponent's side, clogging up their playfield and (hopefully) causing them to lose the match (Hudson Soft 1995b). As the player battles different opponents, the background scenery changes. The background elements are often composed of different layers. However, gameplay (moving and rotating blocks) takes place in a single layer. Interestingly, the "pipes" that make up the border of the playfield are in a layer closer to the camera than the playfield, and it is possible, when a falling piece is still at the top of the screen, to maneuver it such that it is obscured by the UI elements in the top of the screen.

Another slightly different example is *Space Invaders: Virtual Collection* (Taito 1995). In the traditional arcade version of *Space Invaders* (Taito 1978), the aliens are organized in rows that move sideways before moving downwards (when they reach a threshold on either left or right side of the playfield). Virtual Boy's *Space Invaders: Virtual Collection* offers a few different modes and variations for play of the original *Space Invaders* and the arcade sequel *Space Invaders Part II* (Taito 1979) (distributed in the United States as *Space Invaders Deluxe*). These can be played in "original 2D" or in "Virtual 3D."

The "Virtual 3D" mode is the most interesting for our purposes. Here, each row of invaders occupies a different layer, with the invaders closer to top of the screen occupying layers that are further away from the camera in depth and those closer to the bottom placed in layers closer to the camera. This setup is similar to carnival "shooting duck" games where some ducks are further away from the shooter while others are closer. The difference here is that when a row of invaders (or what's left of it) reaches a predetermined position on either side of the screen, the entire row "jumps forward" a layer (toward the player). Unlike the alien invader sprites the player must destroy, the player's ship is always on the same layer. Therefore, this mode's gameplay is affected by the diorama's layers of alien rows. It is harder to target the invaders furthest away because they are smaller on the screen and the player can only act directly in a single layer.

Our final example of a game where the player (mostly) acts directly on a single layer—although there are other layers present that are relevant for gameplay purposes—is *Teleroboxer* (Nintendo R&D1 1995a), a futuristic first-person-view boxing game. Here, the player plays the role of a boxer who remotely controls a robot warrior in a boxing ring against other robots, which in turn are controlled by humans.

The player's robot is represented on screen by its two fists located along the bottom, with most of the rest of the screen occupied by the player's opponent. The layered diorama style is used in the representation of the opponent boxer. The enemies are generally made up of several layers: the closest to the front are the robot's fists, and there are other layers for the head, shoulders, chest/torso, and hips. The robot's layers each move somewhat independently from each other as the robot bobs, weaves, punches, and reacts to getting punched. The effect is quite interesting and reminiscent of paper dolls with articulated limbs—for example, the robot's fists are clearly in front of the rest of the robot.

The player can independently move each of their fists to block or punch, but the interaction with other layers is limited—you can generally hit the opponent's fists or score a hit on the head. As noted, this game is visually striking in its use of different layers to create a single character—a large one that occupies most of the screen—and as such, from the perspective of a diorama, it is somewhat like watching a moving paper doll puppet.

The games with the most sophisticated use of the layered diorama aesthetic are those that use the layers for cosmetic and gameplay reasons, with the player's actions clearly taking place across different discrete layers. The most notable examples of this are *Virtual Boy Wario Land* and *Mario Clash*—both titles developed internally by Nintendo. As *Virtual Boy Wario Land* is described in greater detail in chapter 7, here we will focus on *Mario Clash*.

Mario Clash is a reimagining of the original *Mario Bros.* arcade game (later ported to other platforms). In both *Clash* and *Bros.*, the player must "knock" out all enemies that appear from pipes in order to proceed to the next level. Unlike *Mario Bros.*, in *Mario Clash*, the levels are not flat and two-dimensional. Mario can navigate the space in the game by jumping and moving left and right along ledges. Ledges are often capped (on the left or right side of the screen) with a pipe that Mario can also enter. On entering a pipe, Mario appears on the opposite end of the pipe, and here lies the most significant departure from *Mario Bros.*: the pipes connect ledges at different depths (layers) on the screen. Thus, as in *Virtual Boy Wario Land*, the game's gameplay involves different levels of depth. Unlike *Virtual Boy Wario Land*, there are sometimes more than two levels of depth.

To complete a level and move to the next one, Mario must knock all the enemies off the ledge they are on. To do so, Mario can pick up shells and throw them at enemies. When the enemy is on the same ledge, the effect is similar to the regular Super Mario games. However, Mario is also able to throw shells at enemies on ledges different from the one he's on: flinging them either away from the viewer, toward a ledge further in the background, or toward the viewer and a ledge in the foreground.

As with the other layered diorama–style games, *Mario Clash* is also sprite-based with graphics on multiple layers at different "depths" that provide a parallax illusion that is augmented by the game's stereoscopic screens. And, as expected, the depth perspective is important when flinging shells at enemies on ledges that are at a different depth than the one Mario is currently on.

Mario Clash is a simpler game than *Virtual Boy Wario Land* in that its core gameplay consists of fewer elements. Therefore, we argue that its use of depth—the need to move Mario to a closer/further ledge and to rely on the depth perception to accurately fling shells at enemies—is more significant in this title than it was in *Virtual Boy Wario Land*.

As noted in *GamePro* magazine's coverage, "The graphics have a true 3D feel—Mario throws into the distance, and when he's on an opposite ledge, he throws right into your face" (*GamePro* 1996, 69). *GameFan* magazine similarly remarks how the combination of Mario quality platforming and "3 dimensional gameplay is a perfect marriage" and that the "3D effect is stunning!" concluding with an admonishment that "screenshots will never do this game justice, you've gotta try it!" (Halverson 1995, 58).

We argue that *Mario Clash*'s gameplay is fundamentally designed around making use of different layers—the game even takes place inside a "box" as bounded by the pipes and decorative elements on the left and right sides of the screen, with a brick wall along the far end. The player needs to navigate between different layers while also aiming and throwing shells at enemies—sometimes in the same layer (to the left or right) or into other layers (away or toward the player's view).

The examples we discussed are not exhaustive of the subtleties and nuances in how the layered diorama style appears in Virtual Boy's games. However, they illustrate the ways in which the style is integrated to varying degrees in each title's gameplay. To summarize, we recognize four broad implementations of the layered diorama style based on how the game uses the layered diorama style during moments of gameplay:

- Limited to background or decorative elements, gameplay is not limited to a layer (e.g., *Mario's Tennis*).
- Limited to background or decorative elements, gameplay is limited to a single layer (e.g., *Panic Bomber*).

- Gameplay occurs on a single layer but interacts with other layers in nontrivial ways (e.g., *Space Invaders: Virtual Collection*).
- Gameplay occurs on several layers, and there is nontrivial interaction between the layers as well (e.g., *Wario World* and *Mario Clash*).

There is one last stylistic choice (or variation) that warrants mention: the choice of perspective. If we consider the Virtual Boy as a digital form of a peep box, it makes sense that, for all the games described, the "box" is being looked into from the "side." Sometimes this side view is presented as if from a third-person perspective—in *Golf* and *Mario's Tennis*, there is a character sprite the player can look at while a first-person perspective is used in *Teleroboxer*. There are other games that are instead viewed from the top—a common perspective in video games to be sure but one perhaps less frequently observed in peep boxes. For example, the vertical-scrolling space shooter *Vertical Force* provides the player with a top-down view (figure 5.5) in which players must shoot down waves of enemies, dodge bullets, and evade structures while picking up power-ups. Additionally, players can switch between two layers of gameplay—foreground and background—with the player's ship shrinking in size when it is further away (see figure 5.6). *Vertical Force*'s designers made use of this by creating "multi-tiered stages that require players to move into and out of the background in order to slip around [environmental] structures" such as pillars, beams, and enemy space fortresses (Parish 2021, 60).

Another "top-view" peep box game is *Jack Bros.* In this game, the player controls a character attempting to travel back to the world of fairies by, in a nutshell, getting to the bottom of a six-area "dungeon." Each area consists of a number of floors that must be cleared by finding all the keys on a floor before being allowed to "jump off to the lower floor" (Atlus 1995, 9). The lowest floor of each area has a boss monster that must be defeated in to continue descending.

Jack Bros. makes interesting use of the layered diorama style because while your character may be located on a given floor, the player can in fact see the next floor below. It is shown in less detail, since it is further away, but it does move in relation to the player's current floor (for a bit of parallax effect), and the player can distinguish certain features of the floor below that can play a role in deciding from which point in the current floor to drop down below—for those floors with multiple "drop-down" points. (It's also arguably one of the best games on the system, according to Benj.)

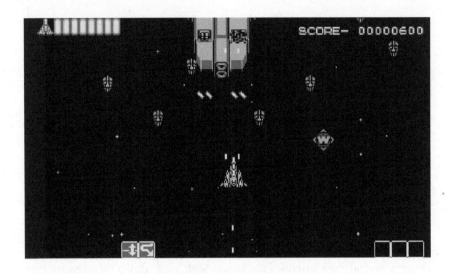

5.5 A screenshot of *Vertical Force* (left eye).

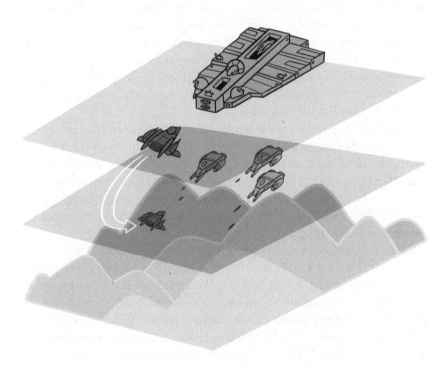

5.6 A recreation of *Vertical Force*'s gameplay layers. Image by Carter Johnson.

Conclusions

We have argued that the Virtual Boy's layered diorama style is an aesthetic of its time due to the technical constraints of the platform (see chapter 4's discussion of the VIP chip). The aesthetic is also the natural result of the incremental progress in expertise in game development accrued through the years: more sprites, more tiles, more ways to move them, and more ways to display them. The Super Famicom, and many of its platform competitors at the time, finally made it easy for games to include multiple backgrounds (layers) and to move them at varying rates from each other. Arguably, the Super Famicom (and the SNES of course), represent a high point in game developers experimenting with the illusion of depth achieved via parallax scrolling. This experimentation naturally continued on the Virtual Boy via the addition of stereoscopic displays but, as we described earlier, incorporating a deeper exploration of ways in which gameplay could be integrated, incorporated, or related to the different layers shown on the displays.

To be fair, this was not a novel concept. Using different layers for gameplay purposes was not unique to the Virtual Boy at the time. Rather, we should consider it an incremental step. Nintendo's *Super Mario World* is an example of an earlier game that made use of gameplay among and between layers. As described by Arsenault and Larochelle (2013), there are areas in the game where Mario, with his back to the player, can climb around on a giant wire fence (e.g., in Iggy Koopa's castle) on which enemies can also climb. The fence also has revolving gates (aka flip panels) that, when punched by Mario, swing around resulting in Mario clinging to the other side of the fence such that he now faces the player. It's a convenient way to avoid enemies on the front side of the fence and/or collect items located behind the fence. Thus, at certain times, *Super Mario World* has multilayer gameplay.

Similarly, the idea of the gameworld as a diorama or a theatrical stage was also explored by Nintendo in its earlier game *Super Mario Bros. 3*. Here the game features a traditional stage curtain in the title screen, and in the game, objects either hang from the ceiling or are bolted to the background—casting shadows on it as well (see figure 5.3 earlier in this chapter, the left screenshot). This conceit, not recognized in the game's manual, was only confirmed by Shigeru Miyamoto many years after the games' original release (Frank 2015). That being said, the visual elements were modified for later releases of the game.

Our argument here is that the Virtual Boy does not represent a stylistic departure from Nintendo's expertise—as much as Gunpei Yokoi hoped the platform would lead to new and distinct kinds of game experiences (Makino 2010b), his ambitions were not fully realized in the game's published softography. Rather, there are hints of new kinds of gameplay via the exploration of gameplay impacting different layers that built on ideas tentatively explored in earlier SNES titles.

To be clear, it was not only Nintendo who was exploring gameplay across layers. *Vertical Force*, described earlier and developed by Hudson Soft, ambitiously furthered some of the ideas explored in the earlier games *Star Soldier*, *Star Force*, and *D-Force*. The former were notable for "their use of layering, allowing players to fly beneath structures within the environment" (Parish 2021, 60), while *D-Force* occasionally allowed the player to "raise and lower [the] altitude" of the Apache helicopter they controlled (Asmik 1991, 7).

We are not arguing that every single Virtual Boy game made use of or featured the layered diorama as their primary visual style (see appendix B for an overview of all the games, including some whose creators opted for a more "realistic" approach). Rather, we argue that the layered diorama style is distinctive and uniquely realized in many of the Virtual Boy's games (in part due to its stereoscopic capabilities).

In all, despite a lack of a major leap forward in either visual presentation or game design innovation, it is somewhat remarkable to consider that the Virtual Boy's ouvre does have a distinct visual aesthetic that results from being able to easily manage multiple graphical layers with a stereoscopic display that doubles down on the illusory depth provided by parallax.

In November of 1994, at the Shoshinkai Software Exhibition in Tokyo, Japan, Nintendo officially introduced the Virtual Boy to the world. The press approached the event with a mix of skepticism and hope—rumors had been swirling for about a year that Gunpei Yokoi, famed creator of the hugely successful Game Boy, was working on a 3D console. Would Nintendo's new hardware be a hit?

Critical reception ranged from tepid to harsh. Ed Semrad titled his editorial of the January issue of *Electronic Gaming Monthly* (*EGM*): "Nintendo Stumbles with Virtual Boy Intro." He doubted that players in the United States would "welcome this new system with open arms" (Semrad 1995, 6). The editors of *Next Generation* magazine called it an "ill-advised 32bit VR system" and wondered if Nintendo had gone crazy (*Next Generation* 1995d, 20).

With the US release months away, and its next major public event due in a few weeks at the Winter CES, things did not look good for Nintendo. Even Nintendo's house magazine, *Nintendo Power*, seemed muted in their coverage of Virtual Boy's reveal. *Nintendo Power* limited its reporting on the Virtual Boy at Shoshinkai to the technical aspects of the console and apologetically pointed out that "the system was shown in prototype form" and "the three game programs shown [. . .] were far from complete" (*Nintendo Power* 1995a, 52).

Nintendo faced an uphill battle to turn what looked like a wave of disappointment and skepticism into a commercial success.

In this chapter, we'll turn our attention to Nintendo's US marketing and promotional efforts leading up to, and following, Virtual Boy's commercial release. By examining the TV ads, print materials (flyers and magazine ads), and the unique (for the time) agreement that Nintendo entered with video rental chain Blockbuster for demoing and renting the console, we can answer questions such as: What was the console positioned as? How was it described, and what was Nintendo attempting to communicate?

In a nutshell, Nintendo's messaging confused consumers by playing against expectations of what "3D" and "virtual reality" could be. Ultimately, Nintendo was unable to clearly position the platform in people's minds, and consumers were not significantly impressed from the experience of renting the device to want to invest in purchasing one directly. But first, let's examine the marketing context in which the Virtual Boy was advertised and released.

Leading up to the Announcement

In the years leading up to the announcement and launch of the Virtual Boy, Nintendo found itself fiercely defending its position as market leader. One of the overarching narratives for video games in the 1990s, now affectionately dubbed "the console wars" (e.g., Harris [2014]), was the struggle for market supremacy between Nintendo and the underdog Sega.

In 1991, Nintendo dominated the video game industry with a US market share of 90 percent (Fitzpatrick 1994), mostly thanks to the NES. However, Sega would soon take a significant portion of that share away. Sega's success during the early 1990s was due largely to its marketing. Sega promoted itself as the edgier alternative to Nintendo. While Nintendo was for children, Sega was for teens. Where Nintendo was safe, Sega was wild. Sega's tagline, famously used in its Sega Genesis advertising, was that "Genesis does what Nintendon't."[1] It worked. By 1994, Nintendo's market share had dropped to 68–71 percent (Fitzpatrick 1994).

Sega's marketing capitalized on the fact that Nintendo's key demographic was, in fact, children and that the children of the NES days were now adolescents looking for new experiences from their electronic entertainment. As Nintendo saw it at the time, the only way to regain its lost market share was to change their tone and address an older audience—the MTV generation.

Nintendo's attempt to rebrand resulted in the "Play It Loud!" campaign that debuted over Fourth of July weekend in 1994. The campaign, described by Billboard magazine as "sharper-edged," was the first time Nintendo would use "brand marketing" (Gillen 1994)—the idea was to communicate Nintendo's (new) core values, increase the value and perception of their brand, and hopefully steal some of Sega's thunder. The campaign's television commercials featured the quick-cut editing style popularized by video music channel MTV together with "cutting-edge music from bands the Butthole

Surfers and Sweaty Nipples." The ads communicated a youthful rebellious attitude using provocative imagery (Gillen 1994, 70).

As part of the "Play It Loud!" campaign, Nintendo released a series of Game Boy models featuring brightly colored cases (not to be confused with the Game Boy Color released in 1998). They also tried to embrace graphic violence in its titles. *Mortal Kombat II* was ported without censorship to the Super Nintendo Entertainment System (SNES), and *Doom*, one of the most notoriously violent video games at the time, also made an appearance on the SNES in September of 1995 in a special red cartridge (Arsenault 2017, 162). As Arsenault notes from examining Nintendo's Spring 1996 catalog, even Nintendo's branded merchandise had changed dramatically. Gone were the Mario pajamas, bedsheets, and lunchboxes. In their place, you could find items like *Killer Instinct* motorcycle jackets (Arsenault 2017, 163).

The overall result of the campaign was, by some accounts, confusing, embarrassing, and awkward (e.g., Arsenault [2017]; Ryan [2011]). For others, it was a success (van de Weyer 2014). The ad agency Leo Burnett USA won a gold Effie award for the campaign in 1995 because it "spoke to kids in a relevant and contemporary way—in their own language, on their own terms [and it] allowed Nintendo to recapture share leadership and gain the number one position in video game sales" (Effie n.d.). Although the campaign appeared to simply copy what Sega had done, it actually "beautifully merged Nintendo's straight-arrow mentality with Sega's edgy attitude" (Harris 2014, 531). Beyond that, Nintendo was successful in positioning itself, and its products, as a valid part of teen culture alongside rock music, skateboards, and BMX bikes (van de Weyer 2014).

While Nintendo's "Play It Loud!" campaign was not designed specifically for the Virtual Boy, the Virtual Boy's campaign would tie into it. Some of the stylistic choices (such as grunge fonts) found in the Virtual Boy campaign originated from the need to align with "Play It Loud!" rather than a quality particular to the Virtual Boy. The Virtual Boy would need to be seen as hip, cool, and edgy to fit in with the campaign, and the language and imagery of its marketing might have to alienate adults and children in order to cater to teens. Virtual Boy would have to be presented as a platform for teens desirous of rebelling against authority.

Marketing the Virtual Boy

On May 11, 1995, Nintendo announced, via a press release, that it would spend more than US$25 million in marketing the Virtual Boy (Nintendo 1995g). This budget would be used to drive interest for the Virtual Boy in the United States with promotional campaigns and events in addition to print and television efforts.

Nintendo's marketing strategy featured three intertwined thrusts. First, it gambled that the only way to convince the public into buying the console was by having them experience it first-hand. We'll call this the "Seeing is believing" thrust of the campaign. Second, it positioned the console as providing a "real" experience distinct from other video game experiences. We'll call this thrust "Real 3D." Third, it communicated that the experience of playing Virtual Boy was immersive in a way no other games were—you were "in" the game. We'll call this the "Immersion" thrust.

Ultimately it was these strategies and messaging that shaped consumers' notions and understanding of what Virtual Boy represented as a platform. As we will see in the end, this might have been a significant factor in the platform's commercial failure: Nintendo was unable to ultimately convince consumers that this was a new platform worth paying attention to.

Seeing Is Believing

One of the more notable commercials Nintendo used to promote the Virtual Boy opened with an off-screen narrator warning.

> It came from the 3rd dimension.
> With its own brain.
> Its own voice.
> Its own legs.
> There's only one problem.
> It needs your eyes.
> Virtual Boy.
> See it now in 3D. (Nintendo 1995h)

The spot opens with an apparently sentient Virtual Boy rising from a cloud of smoke. The camera then zooms forward into the Virtual Boy and cuts to a view, presumably from the inside of the console, from which we see a red-tinted view of a landscape. This view is overlaid with computer-rendered graphics of a targeting reticule with the words "tracking" and a spinning "3-D" in the top-left corner. The camera then quickly focuses on a shaggy-haired youth who turns to flee—the Virtual Boy has located a target. Our view then leaves the "inside" of the Virtual Boy and we see the console pursuing the youth against a smoky yellow background. The Virtual Boy ambles forward on tall spindly metallic legs, tumbleweed underfoot, as its human target leaps away and tries to escape. Too late, the Virtual Boy has locked on, and, now in a first-person camera view, we see a controller shoot toward the human. As the controller reaches its victim, the cord wraps around the human's torso and, conveniently, the controller lands in their outstretched hands. The cord yanks back, the human falls, and their face slides into position inside the Virtual Boy's black neoprene visor. The human is literally a captive audience who cannot look away. The message is clear—the only way to understand what the platform is capable of is to experience it with one's own eyes. It's a forceful and violent image that is tonally aligned with Nintendo's "Play It Loud!" campaign.

The idea that first-hand experience with the platform was the only way to truly understand it was also evident in Nintendo's surprise partnership with NBC and the video rental chain Blockbuster Video. Nintendo had decided to actively support and encourage the rental of its brand-new just released video game platform. Starting on August 14 (launch day) and for a period of about four months, Blockbuster's customers would be able to rent a Virtual Boy packed in a custom hard-shell case and two games of their choice for three days, for only US$9.95.

The deal with Blockbuster was a surprise to many since Nintendo was an ardent opponent of video game rentals (it had helped outlaw the practice entirely in Japan). Nintendo had even tried to bully Blockbuster by suing it in 1989 for copyright infringement—Blockbuster had been renting Nintendo games with photocopies of the manuals (Taylor Jr. 2015). The case eventually settled out of court and was largely seen as a victory for Blockbuster since it continued renting video games.

To be clear, Nintendo had not really had a change of heart regarding video game rentals. Rather, to help their platform succeed, they found themselves bending their own rules. In the words of a Nintendo spokesperson in April of 1994, "We are still in opposition to the concept of allowing video game software to be rented. But the rental business has grown to about a billion dollars annually, or one-sixth the size of the whole US video game industry, and it's obviously an opportunity that didn't make sense for us not to get involved with" (Fitzpatrick 1994, 6). Sega famously endorsed rentals, and it looked like Nintendo was leaving money on the table. So, having failed to succeed in court, Nintendo decided to make the best of a situation it was fundamentally unhappy with.

There was another reason for striking a deal with Blockbuster. Mark Wescott, Nintendo's promotions manager at the time, explained that "Nintendo faced a challenge with the introduction of Virtual Boy—the system that delivers true, 3D graphics can't be demonstrated via traditional marketing methods. [. . .] So, we looked to two leaders in home entertainment—Blockbuster video and NBC—to create an innovative product sampling and sweepstakes promotion to ensure that our audience will experience Virtual

Boy's breakthrough 3D technology first hand" (Wescott, as quoted in *EGM2* [1995], 27). Since Nintendo had decided it needed to get its kit into people's hands, it figured that Blockbuster's network of retail locations and experience in the rental market could provide the infrastructure necessary to get the largest possible number of people to experience the Virtual Boy first-hand.

Nintendo also made the platform available for public demonstrations in stores and at public events. Scheduled over the Labor Day holiday weekend (the first Monday of September), "Virtual Day" allowed the general public in Chicago, Houston, New York, San Francisco, and Atlanta to get their hands on the Virtual Boy (*Electronic Gaming Monthly* 1995a). A similar event billed as the "Virtual Boy Mall Tour" offered the public the opportunity to win promotional giveaways as well as try out the Virtual Boy.

Nintendo reinforced the idea that you needed to see it to believe it with an additional promotion: a sweepstakes. The "Must See 3D Sweepstakes," part of the partnership with Blockbuster and NBC, ran alongside the rental program and included prizes such as baseball caps, Virtual Boy systems, and ten grand prizes. The prizes consisted of a trip to Hollywood and the opportunity to be an audience member at the taping of an NBC show (Nintendo/NBC/Blockbuster 1995). The sweepstakes reinforced the campaign strategy with a clear call to action: "Try It! and then Buy It!" (Nintendo/NBC/Blockbuster 1995). As a way to strengthen this call, the Blockbuster rental program also included a $10 coupon that customers could apply toward the purchase of a Virtual Boy system (which retailed for $179.99).

On September 18, a little over a month after release, Nintendo announced that "40,000 people a day across the country are clamoring to test the system" and that they expected "that more than 1 million people will test the system in the first four weeks of its promotion" (Nintendo 1995a). Exactly one month later, in a press release announcing a US $20 reduction in price, Nintendo asserted that the system was "being tried out by more than 40,000 people per day." They estimated the rental program would reach more than seven million customers by the end of the year (Nintendo 1995b). While the numbers might be suspect, they still serve as an upper bound on the platform's reach via the rental program. If we give Nintendo the benefit of the doubt, the rental program was successful—people rented the console in large numbers—the program only failed because it didn't convince enough renters to follow through with a purchase. Although the plan worked, the premise behind it (that seeing was believing) did not.

Real 3D

The second thrust of Nintendo's promotional strategy was communicating that the experience of playing Virtual Boy went beyond what other video game systems offered. This system, despite the name, was not virtual—it was 3D like the real world.

From a brochure promoting the sweepstakes, we learn that the Virtual Boy "[Is] Not Playin' Around, It's for REAL!" [emphasis in original] and that it features "True 3-D Action," "Incredible Depth and Realism," and "Outrageous New Games in Absolute 3-D" (Nintendo/NBC/Blockbuster 1995). This language extended to the prizes. You could win "totally real prizes from NBC and Nintendo" as well as a "Real-Live VIP trip to Hollywood" (billed as "REAL entertainment"), and the opportunity to "[b]e one of the REAL audience members at the taping of a new NBC show." If you were only lucky enough to win one of the 2,500 baseball caps, you could take solace that "You'll look REAL happening in your Virtual Boy Cap" [emphasis in original] (Nintendo/NBC/Blockbuster 1995).

The intended meaning of the word "real" deserves greater attention. Nintendo eschewed claims of "realism," "verisimilitude," or "authenticity." Instead, they communicated that the Virtual Boy allowed players to experience the virtual environments in games in the same way that we experience the real world: in three dimensions. The tagline used in many television and printed advertisements was "A 3-D Game for a 3-D World." Television advertisements that featured gameplay often included yellow subtitles informing viewers that "When using Virtual Boy®, actual game play [is] in 3-dimensions"(RPGs For Raccoons, 1995).

Nintendo was trying to skirt the distinction between "3D graphics" and "stereographic 3D." 3D graphics describe graphics resulting from the calculations done to three-dimensional representations of geometric data to create 2D images on a screen. Colloquially, "3D" meant on-screen polygons that were rendered and animated in real-time. "Stereographic 3D" meant the sense of depth perception created by viewing two slightly different images with each eye.

Polygonal 3D graphics technologies were cutting edge at the time and were rapidly reaching the home market. In 1994, the Super NES title *Star Fox* used Nintendo's own Super FX chip to great success and acclaim. And Sega utilized its polygonal 3D arcade system boards (starting with the Model 1 released in 1992) to host a variety of innovative polygonal games such as those in Sega's "*Virtua*" series arcade games (*Fighting*, *Racing*, and *Cop* being the most famous).

On the home console front, 3D graphics were a key differentiator for the Sega Saturn (1994) and would see significant mainstream success with the US release of Sony's PlayStation in mid-1995. Also, just around the corner from Virtual Boy's release, starting with Diamond Multimedia's Diamond Edge 3D, consumers would be able to purchase "3D accelerator cards" for their home computers that allowed for "real-time jaw dropping 3D and 2D photo-realistic graphics" (Diamond Multimedia 1995).

In the early-to-mid-1990s "3D" was a buzzword.[2] In 1992, Apogee Software released *Wolfenstein 3D* and kickstarted the first-person shooter genre (four years later, Apogee changed its name to *3D Realms* and released *Duke Nukem 3D*). In 1993, The 3DO Company released its *3DO Interactive Multiplayer* console. From a cursory look at the 1995 US PlayStation launch release schedule, we learn that *Lemmings 3D*, *Power Serve 3D Tennis*, and *3D Baseball '95* should all be available before Q1 '96 (*Next Generation* 1995e). 3D was everywhere.

However, tech companies rarely used the term "3D" to mean stereoscopic depth perception. Thus, Nintendo's quandary: How could they describe the Virtual Boy's graphics in a way that sounded cutting edge while side-stepping the fact that they were typically not polygonal 3D?

By current standards, the cutting-edge 3D graphics of 1994 were crude. It was obvious even then that they did not look at all like things did in the real world. So, Nintendo seized upon the idea that looking at the graphics on the Virtual Boy system is like looking at things in the real world. It was not a gamble that paid off.

Immersion and Altered Perceptions

Nintendo's third thrust was one of immersion: the idea was that when you were playing Virtual Boy, you were inside the game and that the experience would alter your perceptions of the world. In a print ad featuring a dreadlocked young man sitting in a cave with a Virtual Boy in front of him and a controller in his hands, we learn that if you "stick your head in a Virtual Boy [. . .] you won't be the same when you pull it out" and that players should "jump into the Third Dimension and see what it feels like to be inside the game" (Nintendo 1995c).

The act of "entering" the Virtual Boy consisted of, if the ads were to be believed, an acceptance that you were transporting yourself into a new reality and a new state of mind. A print ad explains that "I was passing through a wasteland when suddenly my mind drifted . . . my spirit lifted, my location shifted into a new dimension—a third dimension—a good dimension. [. . .] I stepped into the invention and heard a voice say, turn it on Virtual Boy. A 3-D game for a 3-D world" (Nintendo 1995d). Playing on the Virtual Boy admitted that video game worlds are arbitrary, fantastical, and even nonsensical. "I played tennis with a toad. I was set adrift in the cosmos. I flew into the mouth of a beast. It was just another day in the third dimension" (Nintendo 1995c).

The general message here is confusing. While looking at images in the Virtual Boy is like looking at them in the real world, playing the Virtual Boy

6.1 A Virtual Boy psychedelic advertisement with the tagline "A 3-D Game for a 3-D World" (from *Nintendo Power*, November 1995, rear cover).

is akin to entering an alternate perceptual reality: an altered state of mind; a psychedelic experience of sorts. Several advertisements featured swirling colors and distorted images of the kind associated with drug use and psychedelics. Virtual Boy's US packaging artwork even featured bright colors and photographs in negative with colors reversed into their complementary colors (van de Weyer 2014).

It is unclear if the mind-altering and psychedelic theming was an attempt to appeal to a teenage demographic (e.g., to align with the "Play It Loud!" campaign) or a sly commentary on the notion that video games captivate and "draw players in." While other systems do it metaphorically, the Virtual Boy does it for real.

Despite the budget, the edgy commercials, and the apparent success of the rental program, the platform did not sell in the numbers expected by Nintendo.

While there are many factors that contribute to this commercial failure, the marketing strategy likely played a role as well. To be fair, we should keep in mind that the notion of what a video game platform was (or could be) was being challenged at the time the Virtual Boy was released. An article in the January 1994 issue of *Computer Gaming World* provides an example: "Trying to determine whether the new wave of living room entertainment devices are a legitimate part of computer gaming is a lot like considering whether or not professional wrestling is really a sport" (Miller, Dille, and Wilson 1994). The article examines Philips's CD-I noting how its creator is "no longer ashamed of CD-I as a game machine" and how the device was originally positioned as a "family entertainment" device with no mention of games (Miller, Dille, and Wilson 1994, 66). As soon as Philips saw that "games turned out to be the best-selling titles on the early machine," it changed its approach and began seeking out game developers and tools for broadening the style of games available for the platform (Miller, Dille, and Wilson 1994, 66). The article concludes, after having examined Pioneer's LaserActive system, Commodore's Amiga CD32 (unreleased in the United States), Atari's Jaguar, and the 3DO, that all those systems are essentially computers without keyboards that do not "pose an immediate threat to gaming on the personal computer" (Miller, Dille, and Wilson 1994, 76). Things were getting messy.

In 1994, there were four broad product categories for video games: the arcade machine, the personal computer, the game system (aka game console), and the portable (now handheld). These categories were distinguishable from one another due to their characteristics: display (e.g., display is self-contained, requires a monitor, or uses a television set), the materiality of a "game" (e.g., games come on cartridges or diskettes), and the place where they were enjoyed (e.g., specialized location, home office/bedroom, living room, or on the move). Even the salient or notable technical specifications varied by platform. The number of bits (8 or 16, for example) mattered for game consoles, while the processor speed (in megahertz) and graphics adaptor (EGA, VGA, SuperVGA) were important within the home computer scene.

The distinctions between these market categories, which we might conceive of as a sort of meta-platform, would start to blur in the early 1990s due to technological progress and increased competition.

Two major new consoles were released in 1995: Sega's Saturn and Sony's PlayStation. Together with the 3DO (released in late 1993), these home consoles used CD-ROMs as their primary software medium[3]—a significant departure from the game cartridges that had been the standard way of distributing home console game software since the Fairchild Channel F introduced the concept in 1976, almost twenty years earlier. Simultaneously, multimedia CD-ROMs for use with home computers were starting to take off (Gillen 1995), creating confusion as to what a CD-ROM was for (music, computer software, games, and so on). While a cartridge was clearly something of the realm of the home console and portable forms, the CD complicated matters. So, the materiality of a video game, what a video game was as a physical object, was breaking loose from its market category.[4]

In 1995, Microsoft released a new version of its operating system (OS), Windows 95, to great fanfare and success. Windows 95, with its "Windows Games SDK" (later renamed DirectX), allowed mainstream home PCs to feature and display high-quality multimedia (including games). Windows 95's promise to make hardware device installation and configuration effortless (advertised as "Plug and Play") also extended to games: gone were the days of having to deal with manually edited configuration files and multiple memory management systems. PC games would now be as easy to install and set up as console games were. The home computer was now perceived as a powerful competitor of the home console (Gillen 1995). Formerly distinct market categories for video games were seemingly converging for the first time since the early 1980s, when home computers such as the Commodore 64 often doubled as game consoles.

Furthermore, there were new hardware manufacturers such as Phillips with its CD-I and Turbo Technologies Duo (Schilling 2003). New entrants began experimenting by licensing their technology for others to develop and sell their own machines. Phillips's CD-I was one such technology. Phillips released multiple models of devices across seven different "series" targeting consumers, professionals, and developers. Robert Faber, president of 3DO, described their technology not as a system. Rather, "It's a concept" (Faber as quoted in Miller, Dille, and Wilson [1994, 74]). They did not manufacture devices as they preferred to license their technology to others—again, leading to a variety of machines in different shapes and sizes (arguably, Panasonic's 3DO being the most famous). Here, the hardware was becoming untethered from a technological specification—something familiar in the world of personal computers but definitely unusual in the space of gaming consoles and handhelds.[5]

In a final complication, "a new platform has emerged that is igniting the passions of millions of gamers: cyberspace" (McGowan 1995, 98). Now you could play online—using your telephone to connect your computer to the Internet, a dedicated online service, or another computer. The advent of "online connectivity" was significantly disrupting the way that games could be played, sold, and distributed (witness the rise of "shareware" in the 1980s and early 1990s, e.g., Moss [2022]). Here, we began to see games unmooring themselves from both single locations and a material object—with online play and digitally distributed games becoming increasingly popular.

All of this to say that the Virtual Boy was launched in a moment of overall confusion and uncertainty as to what a video game platform was or could be.[6] This made it hard for Nintendo to establish Virtual Boy as a platform and a potential new market category as Yokoi had envisioned (see chapter 3).

Earlier platforms, like the Sega Genesis or the Game Boy, were not established in a vacuum. They existed in a broader context—a meta-platform if you will—that shaped people's understanding of what they were, how they were used, and what to make of them. Nintendo's Game Boy was a handheld, as was Sega's Game Gear, and thus it was fair and acceptable to compare them as they competed with each other in the same category. The notion of a "portable gaming device" existed before the Game Boy and the Game Gear as well (Nintendo's Game & Watch series and Mattel's series of sports games being the most notable). It is this trajectory, or evolution, that helped establish the "handheld" as a product category. Similarly, early home systems were understood as home versions of arcade games (e.g., from *Pong* to *Home Pong*). And arcade games? They were a new flavor of earlier coin-operated amusement machines—electromechanical games, slot machines, and pinball machines being the most notorious.

So, to what meta-platform could we say the Virtual Boy belonged, or from what lineage could it draw from to establish itself?

It was too far from being seen as a home computer—the lack of keyboard, monitor, and its use of cartridges and batteries made that obvious. It was not an arcade machine—not being coin-operated and supporting multiple games through its use of cartridges made that evident. Perhaps it was a portable? The name of the device definitely put it in the same family as Nintendo's Game Boy, and it also ran on batteries and included a headphone jack. However, it was too large, not "handheld," and was not easily portable—you had to place it on a flat surface to play. Maybe a home game system? It used cartridges but did not support multiple players (a link cable was in development but was never released). It also did not require a television set and had no real place in the living room (dining room table at best), so the play experience was isolating rather than communal. Your friends could not see what you were playing. As discussed in chapter 4, the Virtual Boy's graphical capabilities were comparable in many ways to those of the Super Nintendo: it was "better" in some ways (e.g., more layers that could be scrolled at different speeds for better parallax effects), and "worse" in others (e.g., fewer colors, comparatively worse for Mode 7-style scaling and rotation). However, with six audio channels and limited capabilities for sample-based digitized audio, the Virtual Boy's audio capabilities were closer to Nintendo's Game Boy's synthesized "chiptunes" (four audio channels in the case of the Game Boy and Game Boy Color, Collins 2008, 76) than the Super Nintendo's sample-based capabilities including a "preset stock of MIDI instruments" (Collins 2008, 46), more channels (eight), and 16-bit stereo compared to the Virtual Boy's 10-bit stereo. Journalist Marilyn Gillen described the Virtual Boy as "a midseason replacement" (Gillen 1995). But a replacement for what exactly, for the Game Boy? Or the Super Nintendo?

The other half of the platform's name, "Virtual," definitely connected the system to the broader idea of virtual reality. Accordingly, its industrial design looked similar to virtual reality helmets of the day. This connection was not lost on game journalists. The September issue of *Next Generation* magazine featured a ten-page special report on the current state of VR. The extended article describes the different headsets then available and describes the Virtual Boy as a head-mounted display (HMD) for the masses, despite its lack of tracking (*Next Generation* 1995f). Similarly, *GamePro* magazine argues that with Virtual Boy, Nintendo "turns virtual reality into the real deal" (The Whizz 1995).

We can speculate about how things might have turned out had Nintendo advertised and positioned the Virtual Boy within a meta-platform. It might even have been able to find a place in the meta-platform of virtual reality. The unit definitely evoked the look of a helmet VR unit, and it had 3D stereo graphics. But the system was not head-mounted and lacked any kind of tracking, which might have been seen as too far from what the VR meta-platform was.

Also, within the context of computing, VR was a peripheral. You did not buy a standalone VR system in 1994. Rather, you bought a VR system and hooked it up to your computer.

As we saw in chapter 2, there was a context for stereographic 3D peripherals even in the home console video game space. However, they were never that successful commercially (they had few games and were perceived as gimmicks).

Although video game players were interested in VR, perceptions of the technology tended to skew to the extremes: either as an incredibly exciting thing to look forward to when the cutting-edge technology reached consumer-friendly prices or as a gimmick without much future beyond quick thrills and excitement (see chapter 7). Neither option offered a valuable marketing metaphor for the Virtual Boy, so it might explain why Nintendo chose not to develop a strong connection between VR and the Virtual Boy in their marketing strategy.

What other options did Nintendo have? Nintendo never leaned on the popularity of stereography. The Magic Eye books, featuring autostereographic images that allow people to see 3D images by focusing on specially designed 2D patterns, were incredibly popular in the first half of the 1990s. *Magic Eye: A New Way of Looking at the World* was published in the United States in 1993, and it was quickly followed by two sequels. According to the publisher, the first three Magic Eye books spent a combined seventy-three weeks on the New York Times bestseller list (Magic Eye 2018). In the context of video games, *Magic Carpet*, a 3D game in which players fly around on a magic carpet casting spells, included an autostereogram mode (Clarkson 1995).

Autostereograms also made their way into popular culture, including appearances in television shows. They also appeared in advertising: the October 1995 issue of *Electronic Gaming Monthly* featured an autostereographic advertisement for the upcoming movie *Mallrats* (View Askew Productions 1995). Perhaps Nintendo could have described the Virtual Boy's display in this context?

What is notable about the Magic Eye books is the language they use to describe their content. They are "3D illusions" that present "a new way of looking at the world" (N.E. Thing 1993). The Virtual Boy may have been better served by an association with magic, illusion, and wonder rather than immersion and psychedelia.

Ultimately, Nintendo failed to create a strong perception of the Virtual Boy as a platform. The notion of what it was, why it was interesting, and why it deserved to enter a marketplace that already had three distinct market categories for the video game home consumer was never made clear.

The gaming press remained unconvinced, and, despite the promise of mind-altering experiences, it is possible that consumer rentals simply allowed players to quickly realize that it was not as mind-altering as promised. Its lackluster sales and Nintendo's haste to discontinue it meant that it never really had the chance to establish itself as a platform either. To date, fans still argue about what the Virtual Boy is. Its identity has never existed within a broader meta-platform. It stood alone, a platform of one, undefined and unable to shake its perception as an odd duck, the gimmick(?) that went too far.

The Oxford dictionary defines the modern common use of the word gimmick as "a tricky or ingenious device, gadget, idea, etc. esp. one adopted for the purpose of attracting attention or publicity" (OED Online 2021). Under this definition, video games were, at least in the beginning, gimmicks. The early, and somewhat contested, history of video games is almost entirely made up of "cool tech demos" and experiments used to demonstrate the capabilities of a piece of hardware, show off the technical abilities of their creators, or both. William Higinbotham and his colleagues' *Tennis for Two*, arguably the first video game (Smith 2020), was created to make an exhibit at a 1958 tour of Brookhaven National Laboratory "more dynamic," "give it a little punch," and allow visitors "some 'hands-on' interaction with the hardware" (Anderson 1983, 10). A few years later, DEC corporation enticed potential customers into buying its PDP-1 minicomputer by using the early video game *Spacewar!* to highlight and advertise its capabilities (Smith 2020).

Furthermore, the early years of home video games were ones in which retailers and the mass market press were often confident that these devices were simply a passing fad (Aoyama and Izushi 2003; Goldberg 2011; Herman 2001). That is obviously no longer the case for the industry as a whole. However, to this day, and for good reason, whenever a game company is presenting and discussing the features of its latest device or game, there is always some uncertainty. Which features are gimmicks—simply added to gain attention or provide a distinction over a competitor—and which ones are innovations indicative of future standards? After all, at least in the early days, video games were the "prime harbinger of digital technologies"

(Swalwell 2007, 257), and not all these technologies panned out. Even for incredibly commercially successful game consoles, such as Nintendo's Wii, which retailers had trouble keeping in stock for years after its release, there was talk among industry analysts that it was a fad (Goldberg 2011). Ultimately, this is a discussion and perception that will never leave video games—as cultural artifacts created in an intensely agile and competitive industry making use of the latest technological trends and advances—developing gimmicks to stand out and get attention will always be a part of video games. Historically, in fact, video games are no different than other forms of entertainment media where new products replace the older ones and consumers expect the next game to be better than the last, thus rendering what was once novel and exciting as obsolete at best, junk at worst (Swalwell 2007).

That being said, it can still be useful to examine in what ways and contexts certain platforms and features are conceived of (or not) as gimmicks. And, perhaps due to its commercial failure, the Virtual Boy provides a notable case study to examine.

As we saw in chapter 6, the years leading up to the announcement and release of the Virtual Boy were particularly tumultuous for the video game industry. At the time, a variety of new technologies were creating great uncertainty over what the future of video games could or should be: virtual reality, the internet, polygonal 3D graphics, multimedia computers, and CD rom storage are just a few examples. Which technologies would succeed and what their impact would be may seem obvious to us now, but at the time things were not so clear. Consider the example of LaserDisc games of the early 80s that failed, and then failed again in an attempted comeback in the early 1990s (Wolf 2008b).

In this chapter, we build on Ngai's theory of the gimmick (Ngai 2020) to examine the role of gimmicks in the game industry, the roles they play, and how they are articulated and discussed in the video game press and culture. By understanding some of the subtleties in considering the role of gimmicks in the video game industry, we can explore questions such as: Should we consider the Virtual Boy, as a platform, a gimmick? Is the Virtual Boy's key feature, stereoscopic 3D, a gimmick? We determine that although the Virtual Boy could be considered a gimmick under some lenses, it is ultimately not.

What Is a Gimmick?

In *Theory of the Gimmick* (2020), Ngai provides a perspective on the gimmick that broadens our understanding of the term beyond the mere trick or ploy for attention. Ngai's work highlights several dualities in gimmicks. They are "overrated devices that strike us as working too little (labor-saving tricks) but also as working too hard (strained efforts to get our attention)" (Ngai 2020, 1). They are also the source of both an experience of dissatisfaction (doesn't do quite as advertised) and fascination—we are as much drawn to the gimmick as we are distrustful of its promises. Ngai (2020) notes other dualities: "We call things gimmicks when it becomes radically uncertain if they are working too hard or too little, if they are historically backward or just as problematically advanced, if they are wonders or tricks" (49), and "since the gimmick lies latent in every made thing in capitalism, devices can flip into gimmicks at any moment and vice-versa as well" (5). These dualities are hard to tease apart because "[t]he overperforming and underperforming, grossly overvalued but also dangerously underestimated gimmick's contradictions are inextricably connected" (Ngai 2020, 50). Furthermore, the gimmick does two things as part of its aesthetic experience—it catches your attention only to then relax it once you realize the object is unworthy of that attention (Miller 1990). Gimmicks both create attention and then cause our rejection—undermining themselves in the process.

While Ngai does not discuss video games, we see many of these issues in video games, their hardware, and their underlying technology. In fact, we can use the dualities Ngai identifies as a kind of "lens for appraisal" through which we can examine a platform, game, or feature. For example, when wondering whether—in a particular context—a specific game platform is worthy of the pejorative gimmick, we can ask:

- Does it not do as much as promised or advertised?
- Does it try too hard to get our attention?
- Is it historically backward? or perhaps,
- Problematically advanced?
- Is it grossly overvalued? or maybe,
- Dangerously underestimated?

To be clear, this is not a checklist wherein an affirmative to each question results in a platform being a gimmick. Rather, it provides a roadmap of sorts by which we can explore how (or how not) and in what ways (or not) it is reasonable to consider something a gimmick. This is because, as Ngai reminds us, there is also some relativity in "gimmickness"—both in differences in its perception from person to person as well as in time—for example, something considered a gimmick in the past can be a standard feature in the present.

For example, consider Nintendo's own history with the use of gimmicks (Voskuil 2014) to drive sales of their video game software and platforms. In the mid-1980s, Nintendo was interested in releasing its Famicom platform in the United States. While the Famicom was a commercial success in Japan, things did not look so promising in the United States. Specifically, there was a sense of distrust from retailers having lost money with the so-called "video game crash" a few years earlier (Aoyama and Izushi 2003). This distrust applied to the entire (home) video game industry with the presumption that video games were a fad and that fad had passed. Nintendo decided to draw attention away from the fact that the NES was a game console. After a failed attempt in 1985 at getting interest for the Famicom (presented at the Winter Consumer Electronics Show under the name Advanced Video System), Nintendo regrouped and reconsidered (Altice 2015). They decided to try a new name (Nintendo Entertainment System or NES), offer special deals to retailers in test markets, and bundle the NES with two peripherals: a toy robot named R.O.B. for "robotic operating buddy" and a lightgun (the Zapper). The toy robot, R.O.B., was "the bait that finally caught the industry's interest" (Altice 2015, 96), while Ryan argues it was a twentieth-century Trojan horse designed to hide the fact that the NES was a video game system (Ryan 2011). Nintendo's advertising featured the robot centrally in its promotional materials including TV and printed ads (Altice 2015). Thus, the bait-and-switch of R.O.B. was set: "A robotic playing buddy could divert consumer attention from the NES's core purpose," which was playing video games (Altice 2015, 96).

We can think of the R.O.B. as a gimmick designed to get NES consoles into skeptical retailers' hands and, through them, to consumers. It was advertised as wireless and able to play games alongside players. These statements were technically true but in a roundabout way. The "wireless" feature required that the robot face the TV screen so that it could "see" carefully timed flashes that relayed commands to the robot. There was no way for the robot to communicate with the console other than through the controller. The controller's buttons, when held by the robot, could be pressed following a series of convoluted steps (Altice 2015). So, it did not do quite as much as promised or it did so in a way that was ultimately unsatisfying (i.e., too slow and cumbersome). The robot was also not quite a robot in the sense of being a mechanical entity with some autonomy—it was a mechanical toy disguised as a robot. Overvalued in some ways while undervalued in others: the technology for the NES's communication with the robot was not innovative, but it was simple and implemented efficiently (Altice 2015). Ultimately, "[o]nce players discovered that the NES was an enjoyable console based on the merit of its games alone, R.O.B. was quickly forgotten. After its initial two games, the operating buddy was no longer allowed to play" (Altice 2015, 100). The fact that it was rapidly abandoned (only two games were ever released that supported the robot) strengthens an interpretation of R.O.B. as a gimmick accessory for the NES.

In another example, let's consider Nintendo's Rumble Pak. The device is an accessory for the Nintendo 64 (N64) controller that was first shown publicly in 1996 and publicly released in Japan in April of 1997. The device requires two batteries, is plugged into the N64 controller's memory card slot, and provides haptic feedback while playing video games. This haptic feedback, originally called "rumble" but now more commonly referred to as force feedback, was realized via a single eccentric rotating mass motor (Willumsen and Jaćević 2019). Is "rumble" a gimmick? It was described in the gaming press at the time as "cute, gimmicky—actually kind of fun" (The Lab Rat 1997, 30), "cool"—despite sounding lame (*Electronic Gaming Monthly* 1997, 74), and an innovation that sounded like a bad idea—but was not (*N64Pro* Staff 1997, 64). Arguably, there was suspicion of the Rumble Pak when it was first released. However, that suspicion was dispelled after playing games that made use of it. Furthermore, support for the Rumble Pak quickly became standard for N64 games with Nintendo even rereleasing some games in Japan (e.g., *Super Mario 64* and *Wave Race 64*) to add Rumble Pak support (Harrod 1997). Looking beyond the N64's Rumble Pak, haptic feedback quickly became a standard feature directly incorporated in game controllers, with PlayStation's DualShock controller leading the charge[1] (Murphy 2014).

So, did the Rumble Pack's haptic feedback not do as much as promised? That seems not to be the case. It was neither historically backward nor advanced. Haptic feedback was known in video games for approximately twenty years prior—Sega's arcade motorbike racing game *Fonz: The Game* (1976) was perhaps the first (Wolf 2008a). It was also not problematically advanced as its rapid adoption and continued support shows that, if anything, the timing was just right. Finally, its transition from "extra feature" to standard also signifies that we should not consider the Rumble Pak a gimmick around the time it was released.

These two examples allow us to extend Ngai's lens for appraisal with a few further questions:

- What intention does its producer/creator seem to have?
- What kind of support does it receive from its producer/creator?
- How has its use evolved over time?

Thus, a producer or creator who seems to have the intention of using a feature to draw attention to their product, and perhaps distract from other aspects of its product (e.g., Nintendo's intentions regarding R.O.B.), lends support to an interpretation of the feature being a gimmick. Going further, a producer or creator who demonstrates commitment through continued use and support of the device or feature makes it less indicative of "gimmickness." Here, we can look to Nintendo's support for the Rumble Pack. Finally, we can use the benefit of hindsight to see how a device or feature has impacted what came afterward. Failure to gain traction or widespread use is obviously more indicative of "gimmickness" than the opposite. The fact that the Rumble Pack was an accessory that provided functionality now considered standard in video games does not support considering it as a gimmick.

VB Platform as Gimmick?

Virtual Boy's marketing campaign promised a lot. But did the Virtual Boy not do as much as promised or advertised? Apparently not. While consumers were not overly excited by the platform and the games they played on it—and the rental program was largely successful—no one seems to have argued that the platform did not do quite as much as was promised.

Was the Virtual Boy historically backward or problematically advanced? In many ways, the Virtual Boy was a throwback—its use of single-color red LEDs for powering its display definitely gave it a monochrome look and experience that recalled the early LED-based handheld titles of the 1970's such as Mattel Electronics's *Football* (Newman 2015) and the early days of home computing with the prevalent use of monochrome CRT displays in either green or amber. Furthermore, the graphical resolution was not cutting edge for the time and, at best, reminded people of the Game Boy handheld device that had been realized six years prior. So, in this sense, it was historically backward—it used older technology and failed to achieve results that impressed. Was it problematically advanced? Not really. The only notable contender for an "advanced" design element in the device is its controller—and not thanks to any technical improvements, but rather due to its ergonomic design. Its handlebar "M" shape, allowing a comfortable grip and easy placement of the thumbs on each of the cross-shaped directional pads, was relatively novel for the time though it was preceded by Sony's PlayStation controller released approximately half a year earlier in late 1994. That general controller shape, with comfortable grips for each hand, has since been widely adopted as the "standard."

Perhaps the Virtual Boy, with a US launch price of $179, was misvalued then: it was either too low or too high. Given the issues discussed in chapter 6 regarding its perception, the challenge lies in ascertaining what the Virtual Boy should be compared with in terms of its price and perceived value for that price.

If we compare the Virtual Boy to other handheld devices, we see that, on the lower end, Nintendo's Game Boy (1989) cost $89. However, the Atari Lynx's launch price in 1989 was $179, the same as the Virtual Boy. Sega's Game Gear (1991) retailed for $149, and the Sega Nomad (1995) was priced at $180. So, in the "handheld" category, it's fair to say that the Virtual Boy's price, while not an outlier, was on the higher end of the spectrum. If anything, the Game Boy was an outlier due to its low price. This price differential could be justified because all the handhelds, except the Game Boy, featured color screens. However, in terms of graphical capabilities, the Virtual Boy was comparable to Nintendo's Game Boy due to its monochromatic displays. As Gunpei Yokoi noted, "Color graphics give people the impression that a game is high tech" (Yokoi, as quoted in Kent [2001, 514]). So, the Virtual Boy was not perceived as not "high tech" enough for the price. Was the device's "notable feature" (stereoscopic display) worth double the price compared to the Game Boy? Perhaps not.

We can also compare the Virtual Boy's launch price of $179 (in the United States) to that of home consoles around the same period. The Sega Saturn (1995) cost $399 at launch. Sony's PlayStation retailed for $299 when it launched in the United States in 1995, while the upcoming Nintendo 64 (1996) was only $199. In this category, the Virtual Boy's price was low. The Virtual Boy was, stereoscopic displays aside, graphically much less impressive than the home consoles but did not require a TV set to play. In all, we could say that the Virtual Boy was priced appropriately for a home console device—it was worse in terms of features but also comparatively cheaper.

A final point of comparison should consider the price of consumer-grade VR systems and peripherals. In 1993, VictorMaxx released the StuntMaster for $219.95 (VideoGameKraken n.d.). The device was a head-mounted display that served as a peripheral for the Super Nintendo and Sega Genesis consoles. While the price is comparable to Virtual Boy's, the StuntMaster was a peripheral that required consumers to invest in the home console. The CyberMaxx, released as a sequel of sorts to the StuntMaster, was an upgraded system that addressed the critiques of the poor-quality displays and resolution in the StuntMaster. However, its entry-level model cost $699, and it was designed to connect to home computers rather than game consoles (VideoGameKraken n.d.). Another company, Virtual i-O, released the Virtual i-glasses for $599 (without tracking), while Forte Technologies's VFX1 system listed for $995 and was bundled with a CD with demo versions of popular games at the time and promised support for many more (Youngblut et al. 1996). Compared to these devices, the Virtual Boy's price point is low—perhaps in the "too good to be true" category for a VR device. All of the VR devices listed previously also required additional investment in either a high-end computer or a game console. The Virtual Boy was obviously worse in terms of graphical capabilities (monochrome and low resolution), it didn't feature head tracking, and it was not head mounted. So, the Virtual Boy as a "standalone" VR device definitely seems misvalued (too cheap) even if consumers were not fully aware of its features (or lack thereof). But was the Virtual Boy's price too good to be true?

We can compare the Virtual Boy with another platform: Tiger Electronics's R-Zone. "What's red and black, has a controller and cartridges and provides a gameplay experience most people have never seen before in their life?" (*Electronic Gaming Monthly* 1995b, 26). The article in *Electronic Gaming Monthly* continues "Virtual Boy? Sure, but now there are two answers to that question" (*Electronic Gaming Monthly* 1995b) They continue describing the R-Zone as a device that "appears to be a full-fledged system" with a "screen and speaker [that] are housed in a small box that you strap on your head. Connected to the box is a multi-button controller" (*Electronic Gaming Monthly* 1995b). The R-Zone uses cartridges, and there are several games available for purchase such as *VR Troopers* and *Virtual Fighter*. However, the device's screen is contained in the game cartridges and consists of a transparent (see-through) LCD with predrawn graphics that are then "activated" such that they are seen as needed during gameplay. The graphics themselves don't move, but rather they are turned on/off. The display fundamentally uses the same technology seen in Nintendo's Game & Watch handheld games but on a smaller screen and with more detailed graphical elements. Curiously, the games are displayed using a dark red color and are viewed by the player on a transparent lens that is held in front of one of the players' heads (thanks to the headband). Despite not having any of the features you would expect from a VR system, it was still described as a "miniature virtual-reality system" (*Electronic Gaming Monthly* 1995b, 26) selling for the super-cheap price of $29.99.

If forced to pick between the Virtual Boy and the R-Zone to decide which platform better deserves to be called a gimmick, the answer is obvious. The R-Zone fails to deliver a remotely adequate player experience. Reviews advised that it was "a waste of time and money" and should be "dumped into the trash can where it belongs" (Jones 1995). It did not help that the system's games were "low-quality" (Herman 2001, 241), and, while both platforms had red-shaded displays, the R-Zone's "aren't even in the same league as the Virtual Boy's" in terms of providing an immersive play experience (*Electronic Gaming Monthly* 1995b, 26). The R-Zone is a cheap platform with mediocre games and gameplay that was dated at the time it was released, all while looking like something it was not—a VR system. From this view, as a VR-lite system, the Virtual Boy does not seem like a gimmick platform at all.

We should also examine how the platform was supported by Nintendo. Nintendo's R.O.B. for the NES was a gimmick partly because there was never any significant support for it—only two games were released that made use of the robot. While the Virtual Boy's officially released titles number only twenty-two, Nintendo was committed to releasing titles for the platform on a regular basis—one a month immediately after the system's launch according to an interview with Gunpei Yokoi (*Next Generation* 1995a). Nintendo developed and published five of the twenty-two titles for the system, two of which were release titles both in Japan and the United States (*Mario's Tennis* and *Teleroboxer*). Of Nintendo's own titles, two feature their most famous and valuable intellectual property: Mario (*Mario's Tennis* and *Mario Clash*). A third title, *Virtual Boy Wario Land*, featured Wario—who, while not as popular at the time as he is now, was nonetheless an important character in the "Mario Universe." Wario was featured as the antagonist in *Super Mario Land 2: 6 Golden Coins* (1992) for the Game Boy and as the playable protagonist in *Wario Land: Super Mario Land 3* (1994) for the same platform. More importantly, reviews for Nintendo-developed Virtual Boy games were generally not poor—ranging from mixed (some good, some bad) to mostly positive. Therefore, it is hard to argue that Nintendo did not support its Virtual Boy platform by not developing any quality games for the system or using any of its valuable characters (e.g., Mario). In terms of its support, perhaps the most damning critique would be that Nintendo was purposefully shy about recruiting support from third-party developers (*Next Generation* 1995a).

Evidence supports the notion that considering the Virtual Boy platform as a gimmick is unfounded and perhaps a bit unfair. The platform was reasonably priced (in several contexts), was adequately supported, and didn't significantly under-deliver. It just wasn't a "winner"—no one was particularly impressed by it, which runs counter to the idea of the platform being a gimmick. Gimmicks at least get attention!

So, why does the Virtual Boy seem to have a reputation as a gimmick? Perhaps this has more to do with how it was referred to after it had failed to succeed commercially.

When Nintendo announced the 2014 release of its Nintendo DS handheld game console, there was concern in the video game press. The Nintendo DS was announced as an experimental product that would sit alongside, instead of as a successor to, the Game Boy Advance (GBA) handheld that was current at the time. *Games* magazine's staff writers expressed that "There's also a nagging doubt that the DS is little more than a gimmick—something to keep the crowds occupied until the true successor to the Game Boy Advance appears" (*Games* 2004b, 7). Similarly, *Cube* magazine noted that "Nintendo have their work cut out to convince the wider world of games players that the system offers something new and enduring and not just a gimmick" (*Cube* 2004a, 34). The "gimmick" here referred to the Nintendo DS's distinguishing feature: its two screens, with the lower one being a touchscreen.

The concerns about the Nintendo DS were often presented using the Virtual Boy as a point of reference and comparison: "The DS could become the Virtual Boy of the 21st Century" (*Cube* 2004c, 14), "The poorly designed DS seemed more show than go, relying on lesser 3D technology than the Sony [PSP handheld] and a gimmick that makes the Virtual Boy look like a cure for the common cold" (Halverson 2004a, 52). Over the years, the Virtual Boy has regularly been used as an example of a platform-as-gimmick. For example, *Australian GamePro* magazine commented on rumors regarding the then-announced Nintendo Wii console by stating that "Nintendo are definitely outside 'the box' on this one, and they better hope that the world wants to play games in different ways *cough* Virtual Boy* cough*" (*Australian GamePro* 2004, 8).

While we do not believe that the Virtual Boy as a platform was a gimmick, we cannot argue with the fact that it was often presented as such—especially in the years that followed its cancellation as new platforms were announced and presented. It is an easy example to refer to when discussing new video game platforms that purport to innovate or include novel features. After all, the Virtual Boy was trying to innovate and it was deemed a commercial failure by its creators. Perhaps that was the Virtual Boy's weak point—it was trying to broaden the design space and possibilities for video games. As the platform's creator noted, "I think game companies ran out of new ideas. I wanted to create a new kind of game that was not a video game, so that designers could come up with new ideas" (Yokoi as quoted in Kent [2001, 514]). Dave Halverson, editor-in-chief of *Play* magazine, explains further, "While many have already branded the DS a gimmick hearkening back to the ill-fated Virtual Boy, I beg to differ. In the first place, the Virtual Boy had amazing potential. The games the world never saw that we had access to early on would have made all of the difference (there's still nothing like them available), but Nintendo pulled the plug—back when Sega made doing so fairly routine—due to either lackluster sales (which they weren't) or some kid in Japan who walked into a ditch (depending on who you talk to). What I like about Virtual Boy (I play Wario World and a handful of other VB games on a regular basis) and now the DS is the way Nintendo strives to evolve the gaming experience—actually change it—rather than merely making prettier games and piling on non-gaming functionality" (Halverson 2004b, 4).

Platform Features as Gimmick

While we have argued that the Virtual Boy as a platform is undeserving of the moniker "gimmick," we should also consider whether the platform's signature feature, its stereoscopic display, should be considered a gimmick. To do so, we will examine some of the Virtual Boy's published games to see how they used its stereoscopic display.

Before getting into how stereo was used in some of Virtual Boy's games, it might help to have some context as to how the term gimmick is used by the video game press when reviewing or discussing games. Broadly, when a game has a distinct feature or element, it is described as a gimmick when that feature is either perceived as unimportant to the game's core experience or somehow detracting from it. For example, consider Konami's Game Boy Advance game *Boktai*: "The original Boktai introduced a neat little gimmick to the usual fare of boy against vampires. Instead of a stake or a bottle of holy water, Django, a spiky-haired RPG-looking dude, was armed with a light-sensitive solar pistol. The GBA cart had a sensor that used sunlight to charge up your light beam. It was a neat little trick, but slightly pointless if you lived in a typically cloudy British town" (Burman 2004). Similarly, "[a]lthough the sunlight element is interesting, it ends up being a bit of a gimmick and means that you're restricted to certain times of day to play effectively" (McChoke 2004). Here, *Boktai*'s sunlight sensor is described as a gimmick due to its perceived negative effect on the gameplaying experience.

We contrast this with *Kirby's Tilt 'n' Tumble*, a Game Boy Color game whose cartridge included a built-in accelerometer, allowing players to control the titular character by moving and tilting the handheld. "Don't be fooled into thinking this is just a gimmick. It's an integral part of the gameplay, which is so refreshingly original and highly innovative that you just can't help but love every aspect of this incredibly entertaining title" (*Future* 2001). Also, in *Goblin Commander*, players could take control of a giant Titan unit: "Admittedly, when we first heard about this particular feature we worried it was nothing more than a gimmick, but once again Jaleco has got it right. Far from a throwaway feature, taking charge of Titans actually serves to draw you into the game by giving you a more active role" (*Cube* 2004a; 2004b). Or, in another example, "The ability to 'sight-jack,' or see through the eyes of your enemies [in PlayStation 2 game *Forbidden Siren*[2]], could easily have been nothing more than a flashy gimmick, but thanks to clever integration this genuinely creepy ability is absolutely essential" (*Games* 2004a).

So, was the use of stereo 3D important, detrimental, or irrelevant to the Virtual Boy's games? Rather than analyze each of the Virtual Boy's games, we'll focus on two titles and how reviewers described their use of stereo 3D (for more on this, see chapter 5). Specifically, we will focus on two games that were praised for their use of stereo 3D. In doing so, we will argue that, since there are at least a few games for which stereo 3D was notably used, we should not consider "Stereo 3D" a gimmick feature for the Virtual Boy.

Virtual Boy Wario Land

Virtual Boy Wario Land was developed by Nintendo R&D1 and released in the United States in December of 1995 (Nintendo R&D1 1995b). The game stars Wario as he decides to gather/steal treasure after finding a hidden cave while vacationing in the "Awazon" river basin (Nintendo 1995i). The game is a sprite-based side-scrolling platforming game in which Wario can jump, charge, and throw enemies and objects. Additionally, Wario can find and wear hats that provide additional powers. The game consists of a series of levels, including boss fights, that the player must progress through by finding the key to unlock an elevator to the next area.

Generally, the game is presented via several layers of graphical elements: a foreground and multiple backgrounds. When Wario moves, the layers also move (scroll) but at different speeds, giving the illusion of depth (parallax scrolling). This parallax effect is more visually compelling thanks to the stereoscopic display. Also, as Wario navigates an area, it is common to see game objects in a background layer—for example, blocks and coins—that are reduced in size because they are further away. One of the game's signature gameplay elements is the ability to (when standing on "jump boards") jump "back" (away from the player/camera) into these background layers (see figure 7.1). Once there, the player controls a reduced-in-size-on-the-screen Wario (because he's further away) who can destroy blocks, collect coins, and so on. Jumping when on a "jump board" while away results in Wario jumping into the foreground—or main area of play (see figure 7.2).

The use of foreground/background is arguably one of the game's main gameplay themes. Wario's jumping away/toward is used in other areas such as one of the optional mini-games available between levels. Additionally, there are enemies and hazards whose cyclical movement patterns occur along the "close/far" axis. For example, spiked balls suspended with chains swing forward/backward instead of the usual left/right pattern seen

7.1 Wario jumping between foreground and background gameplay layers with additional non-gameplay layers. Image by Carter Johnson.

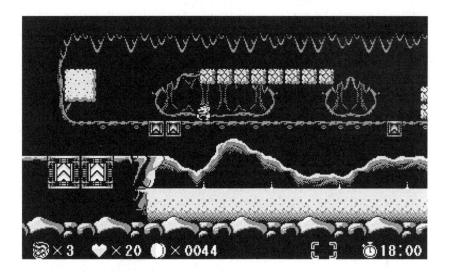

7.2 Wario walking toward a jump board that allows him to jump toward the foreground gameplay area.

in other platform games. Some enemies, for example a small fish in level 3, swim from the background (safe for Wario) to the foreground (unsafe).

Strictly speaking, none of these gameplay elements require stereoscopy. However, they are all designed to the strengths of a stereoscopic view—the illusion of depth. Therefore, the game's central gameplay is enhanced thanks to its stereoscopic display. For example, it is harder to avoid hazards that move toward/away from the screen without the benefit of a stereoscopic display. *Nintendo Power* notes how in this game the "Virtual Boy's ability to create a sense of depth and distance [. . .] isn't just a gimmick that screams, 'Hey look! 3-D!'"; they argue that "[l]eaping between the foreground and background becomes an integral part of the run-stomp gameplay" (*Nintendo Power* 1995c, 36) and summarize noting that the game "shows off all that the Virtual Boy can be" with "excellent use of 3-D graphics and elements" (*Nintendo Power* 1995b, 106). This sentiment was echoed in other reviews at the time. The background/foreground mechanic was even studied by, and inspirational to, other game developers including Retro Studios for their game *Donkey Kong Country Returns* (*IGN* Staff 2011) and Renegade Kid's Nintendo 3DS title *Mutant Mudds*: "The layer jumping on that game [*Wario World*] was definitely the inspiration for Mutant Mudds' layer jumping" (designer Jools Watsham as quoted in Dillard [2012]).

We should not consider the use of stereo 3D a gimmick in *Wario Land* because it is used in a way that reinforces and strengthens the game's central gameplay theme: movement between foreground and background. Even reviewers who noted that "the ability to leap forward and backward in the 3D plane does little to add to the actual gameplay" recognized that *Wario Land*'s designers "actually incorporate the Virtual Boy's 3D capabilities into the game" (*Next Generation* 1995d). Arguably, Nintendo R&D1 chose foreground/background movement and gameplay specifically to play to the Virtual Boy's strength.

Red Alarm

Perhaps stereo 3D is a gimmick when its addition is limited merely to providing a "better" gameplay experience? So, we should examine a title that in practice is rendered mostly unplayable without stereo 3D: *Red Alarm*.

Red Alarm is a space shooter in which the player controls a spaceship in a 3D environment and must fly around shooting enemies and avoiding hazards (T&E Soft 1995c). The game's programmer/designer Mitsuto Nagashima commented that "at that time, there already seemed to be a lot of enthusiasm for developing three-dimensional shooting games," and he "wanted something that could only be done in 3D" (as quoted in Szczepaniak [2015, 64, 65]).

Unlike most Virtual Boy games that used 2D sprites, *Red Alarm* uses wire-frame polygonal 3D graphics for the player's ship, enemies, visual effects, and environmental features (e.g., walls and openings). Additionally, the game features four different camera views for the player to select from, including a cockpit view, ¾ top-view, and two different "behind-the-ship" views that allow players to see enemies that are behind them.

As you would imagine, the stereo 3D allows for easier navigation and flying, with the player better able to tell which enemies are further away, and so on. In this sense, especially when in cockpit mode, the game is no different from any modern 3D space shooter. Therefore, it might seem ludicrous that this game is only playable thanks to the Virtual Boy's stereoscopy. Stereo is crucial for this game for three reasons. First, the game screen is often filled with enemy ships, environmental elements, and more. Second, due to the wire-frame graphics, all of the game's elements are effectively transparent—objects in the world are not really occluded by those closer to the camera. Third, Virtual Boy's monochromatic color palette makes it challenging to make use of atmospheric perspective (also called aerial perspective)—a technique where the illusion of depth is created by modulating the color of an object based on how far away it is.[3] This results in the game screen being incredibly challenging to make sense of, especially when in motion, without the benefit of stereo 3D: it all looks like a jumbled mess of lines. The game's designer/programmer explains, "I added the ability to tweak the parallax effect in the game's options menu. [. . .] At depth level 0, I couldn't play the game at all. Not only couldn't I play it, but I couldn't even tell what was happening in the introductory movie! The impact of the 3D was far greater than I'd ever imagined. I took that as proof that I'd succeeded in making *Red Alarm* a game that could never have been made if it weren't for the Virtual Boy" (Szczepaniak 2015, 68).

Although reviewers at the time commented that the wire-frame graphics were often confusing and hard to make sense of, the game was only playable thanks to the depth perception that helped players better understand when, for example, an enemy was in front of the player's ship rather than behind it. Therefore, due to the computational limitations of the Virtual Boy (e.g., challenges of rendering real-time solid 3D graphics rather than wireframes), stereo 3D is not a gimmick in *Red Alarm*.

Final Thoughts on Stereoscopy and Gimmicks

We have examined two of the Virtual Boy's twenty-two commercially released titles to determine whether, in their game design, they made use of the particular affordances that made the Virtual Boy notable as a platform.

We have done so to answer the question of whether the Virtual Boy's stereoscopic display, as a feature, should be considered a gimmick. Our argument is that, since there are games that made use of this feature in a meaningful and significant way, it would not be fair to consider the features a gimmick. Had we been unable to do so, our argument that stereo 3D is not a gimmick would not hold.

However, as we conclude this chapter, it is important to pause and remind ourselves of the way in which we've been using the term gimmick. Could we argue that stereo 3D, not just in the Virtual Boy but in all of the platforms that have been developed and commercialized since, will always be a gimmick?

In chapter 2, we discussed how all of the currently known technologies for stereoscopy are fundamentally about tricking the human eye into the perception of depth when there is none. The basic concept that makes the illusion "work" is to show the human eye two different flat images that the brain then processes and creates the illusion of depth (which may be stronger or weaker depending on the original images, of course). However, there is a fundamental problem with these images—although some elements depicted in them may appear closer and others further away, the images themselves are static and can never change based on what the viewer's eye focuses on.

Try the following. Hold your hand out in front of you—an arm's length away and with your fingers spread out. Now, focus your eyes on your hand. While focused on your hand, you can still see things that are behind your hand and between your fingers. However, assuming they are far enough away, they will appear blurry and out of focus. Now, without moving your hand or your eyes, focus on something in the background between your fingers. Now that your hand is blurry and out of focus, you might even "see" more fingers than you actually have. This happens because we can focus our eyes on objects that are at different distances. However, this is (currently) impossible to do in any game that uses stereoscopy. If things are blurry and out of focus, it is because they have been rendered or photographed that way—you cannot focus your eyes on the background between your virtual hand's fingers and have the virtual fingers blur. Everything is always focused (unless explicitly rendered otherwise). This might change with new technologies—for example, VR systems such as PlayStation's PSVR2 include eye-tracking, allowing for foveated rendering (Nishino 2022). This is a technique currently used primarily as a way to reduce computational processing by reducing the image quality in a viewer's peripheral vision (Patney et al. 2016). We can envision variations of this technique used to simulate the eye's ability to focus on objects at different distances by purposefully blurring objects that are significantly closer or further from the one the eye is focused on.

However, does this mean that, until we are able to adjust the graphics displayed on a screen based on what we know the viewer's eyes are focusing on, any form of stereoscopy (using technologies currently known) is a gimmick?

This is a book about perception: how we think of platforms by considering our perceptions of them as well as what they help us perceive or—as in the case of the Virtual Boy and its stereoscopic displays—misperceive. Over the course of this book, we have looked at how the Virtual Boy is part of a tradition of visual entertainment devices that use optical tricks and illusions to immerse their audiences. This tradition predates video games and includes the peep box and similar devices. Specifically, we argued that the Virtual Boy is a digital peep box in two key aspects: (1) how it visually immerses its users and (2) its visual signature, the layered diorama. We also discussed how the Virtual Boy was developed with a particular vision: Gunpei Yokoi's desire for a new kind of video game entertainment experience—one with "a totally dark viewing field" that "made it possible to represent an unlimited distance" (Yokoi and Makino 2010, 163, 164). Everything discussed previously relates to and addresses how the Virtual Boy directly affects our perception—what we perceive with our eyes and the feeling of immersion that results from using it.

We also looked at perception from a different perspective. We examined how Nintendo attempted, through its marketing efforts, to position the Virtual Boy in the eyes of its intended consumers: in other words, how Nintendo tried (and ultimately failed) to create a perception of its latest device as something exciting and desirable that opened new arenas and opportunities for video game play. The mid-1990s were a tumultuous time for the game industry, and people's perceptions of what a gameplaying device could or should be were shifting and changing as technological breakthroughs upended past platform categories (e.g., handheld, console, PC, and so on). We argued that consumers were confused as to what kind of device the Virtual Boy was, unsure of what to make of the device, and unconvinced by their hands-on experiences with it. By mid-1996, Gunpei Yokoi opined that "If Nintendo came out and advertised that the Virtual Boy was *not* for gamers, I think that could rekindle people's interest"[1] (Eno 1996). The problem, in Yokoi's eyes, was that it was poorly received by "hardcore gamers" whose complaints negatively influenced other gamers—while the kids and "regular people" who played "really enjoyed it" (Eno 1996). Years later, Shigeru Miyamoto also claimed that Nintendo made a mistake in how they presented the Virtual Boy. Had they presented it as a toy rather than a gaming platform, it would have been perceived differently by consumers and been considered a success by Nintendo (Iwata 2011). Customers were, in the end, not persuaded that the Virtual Boy allowed for novel and exciting video game experiences. It was not perceived as new, flashy, cutting edge, or technologically impressive. It was perceived as neither desirable nor convenient to use and play. If anything, it was perceived as disappointing and potentially dangerous as rumors and reports that it caused headaches took hold.

Perhaps the platform was simply perceived (or, as its fans might argue, misperceived) as a gimmick: designed around a novelty that seemed to offer something of value but was ultimately just a trick. We showed how the video game industry, like other creative industries (Balland, De Vaan, and Boschma 2013), has always valued the importance of novelty (with an interest in leveraging it for financial and commercial success). The "gimmick" in the game industry is not necessarily a bad thing and has been used successfully as a commercial and development strategy countless times. Nintendo itself had significant experience with gimmicks prior to (and some would argue also after) the development of the Virtual Boy. While we argue that the Virtual Boy's reputation as a gimmick is unwarranted, holding this view puts us in a minority. However, we note that this reputation is not quite contemporaneous to the Virtual Boy's release: we most often see it appear a few years after the Virtual Boy's cancellation in the video game press. The perception of the Virtual Boy as a gimmick was created both to explain its commercial failure and as a cautionary tale for newer upcoming platform releases such as the two-screen Nintendo DS released in 2004. To this day, despite a resurgence in interest in virtual reality, we cannot fully escape the idea that stereoscopic gameplay, the Virtual Boy's defining feature, is more about style than substance—especially when divorced from other functionality such as head tracking.

As we wrap up this book, we thought it would be important to briefly consider the present-day perceptions of those who consider themselves fans of the Virtual Boy. What is the source of their fandom and passion, and in what ways can we distinguish it from similar video game fandoms? In what ways does their perception of the platform differ?

Nostalgia

We have never seen, or heard of, people wistfully staring at the horizon as they recall joyful moments they experienced playing on their Virtual Boys while growing up. While we are sure that such fans exist, they are probably few in number. Unlike other platforms, it is harder (but not impossible, of course) for those who currently cherish the Virtual Boy to explain their feelings toward the platform in terms that allude to nostalgia: an idealistic vision of past, full of generally youthful and potentially transformative play experiences. An apparent lack of nostalgia for the Virtual Boy might be surprising considering the increasing importance that nostalgia has in video games (Taylor and Whalen 2008). Video game nostalgia is, to an extent, generational—it largely began in the 1990s and looked back to games from twenty years prior: the 1970s (Esposito 2005). This nostalgia has since grown by leaps and bounds, slowly including more recent games and platforms: the 1980s, 1990s, and beyond. Video game nostalgia has also been commercialized and labeled as retrogaming. Nowadays, it is possible to easily play many older games via emulation, compilations adapted for current platforms, conversions, updates, remasters and more (Thomasson 2014). For those desiring to play from their original game cartridges, there are modern retro-consoles that emulate the original ones or recreate their functionality entirely by using field-programmable gate arrays (FPGAs) (e.g., Hyperkin's RetroN video game console series, and Analogue's Analogue Nt, Pocket).

The commercialization of video game nostalgia has largely ignored the Virtual Boy. Perhaps it is a simple numbers game. Due to its relatively low sales (that still numbered in the hundreds of thousands of units) and somewhat limited release, the Virtual Boy is too "rare." Not enough people encountered it in their youth, and therefore there is not enough nostalgic demand for its games to be rereleased or ported to other platforms (e.g., Nintendo's auto-stereoscopic 3DS handheld).

That being said, there is a small but highly active and productive Virtual Boy fan community. As is common for other video game platforms, there are multiple Virtual Boy emulators, fan sites offering commentary and information, active homebrew development projects (including multiple released titles, far more than were ever commercially published), hardware mods allowing connection to TV sets/monitors, add-ons (e.g., multi-game flashcarts and handcrafted arcade joysticks[2]), and more.

The Virtual Boy fan community can be broadly characterized as coalescing around three practices: (1) collecting, playing, and enjoying the platform's commercially released games; (2) discovering and restoring unreleased games; and (3) developing new games and hardware for the platform (Mora-Cantallops and Bergillos 2018). Therefore, it would be unfair to characterize Virtual Boy fandom as rooted in, or driven by, nostalgia. If nostalgia is cherishing a past that was, or at least an idealized perception of that past, then Virtual Boy fandom is better characterized as driven by an interest in a future that could have been. In other words, a lot of the work done by the Virtual Boy fan community wrestles with the perception that the platform was never allowed to achieve anything near its full potential: it is the underdog that never got its chance to shine. What could the Virtual Boy have been like had its release not been rushed due Nintendo's desire to release it as a stopgap for its delayed Nintendo 64? What might have happened had it not been canceled so surprisingly swiftly? Could it have been a "slow burner" game platform that slowly but steadily accrued players as more titles were released? Was, perhaps, one of the several announced but ultimately unreleased games a "killer app" that could have convinced everyone that this strange and unusual platform was, well, "good"?

Most video game platform fandoms have the benefit of being based on a device that experienced what is described as a full product lifecycle: platform sales increasing over a few years before slowly declining as the technology is perceived as obsolete and consumers begin to anticipate the next "generation" platform (Marchand 2016). The game platform lifecycle also considers improvements in the games released. As developers gain experience and knowledge with the platform, including things that could have been done better in earlier titles, they are able to better take advantage of its affordances. The Virtual Boy had no such luxury, so we see fans engaging in projects and activities that, arguably, create a potential alternate past (and present) for the Virtual Boy. This alternate timeline "restores" what could or should have been milestones in the platform's lifecycle. We will show notable examples of fan-driven research and activities that illustrate this interest in an alternate past for the platform.

Nintendo's Virtual Boy development manual includes details on the device's "communication port [that] is used to communicate between Virtual Boy units" (Nintendo 1995e, 4-4-13). Communication between Virtual Boy units requires the use of a special cable, advertised as the "Virtual Boy Game-Link Cable" in the platform's US instruction booklet (Nintendo 1995f,

26). The cable was scheduled for release in early 1996 (*Electronic Gaming Monthly* 1995c) but ultimately never shipped.[3] In 2010, fifteen years after the Virtual Boy's release, *Planet Virtual Boy*[4] user DogP announced plans for creating a Virtual Boy GameLink cable and polled the community regarding their interest in such a project (DogP 2010). Over the next couple of years, DogP iterated on the design of the cable, posted updates on the prototyping process, discussed features and possibilities with community members, and uploaded pictures of the cable's work-in-progress. In mid-2017, Kevin Mellott (mellott124 on *Planet Virtual Boy*) announced that he had picked up the project (with a new design) and that prototype cables would be forthcoming to interested VB homebrew developers, and the first handful were shipped a few weeks later (Mellott 2017). As Virtual Boy user speedyink commented, "Finally, we can experience one of the key features Nintendo should have included at launch, 22 years later!" (speedyink 2017).

Curiously, homebrew support for the cable link predates the availability of a physical cable for fans to purchase. This support was implemented in some of the platform's emulators and utilized in a handful of homebrew games and projects. The most notable of these is *Hyper Fighting* (Mr. Anonymous 2013) released a few years after DogP's announced GameLink cable project. *Hyper Fighting* was intended as a homebrew version of *Street Fighter II Turbo: Hyper Fighting* (Capcom 1992) for the Super Nintendo Entertainment System (Stevens 2015). The game was well received in the Virtual Boy community and even saw a limited release on a custom cartridge with a cardboard box and printed game manual. Considering that the game was based on the SNES port of the original *Street Fighter II* arcade game, *Hyper Fighting* serves as a plausible example of what Capcom might have released for the Virtual Boy in 1995: a game that could have made a difference in the platform's success.

In 2017, some weeks before Mellott's GameLink cable announcement (2017), *Planet Virtual Boy* user M.K. announced that unused GameLink functionality had been found in a disassembled version of *Mario's Tennis* source code (M.K. 2017). Additionally, M.K. was able to restore two of the three disabled game modes (player vs. player mode and player + computer vs. player + computer) and provided a patch that could be applied to the game to restore the aforementioned functionality (M.K. 2017). Here, finally, was a version of *Mario's Tennis* that demonstrated what the game was presumably intended to have been like when it was released alongside the Virtual Boy.

These are two examples of the Virtual Boy fan community speculating on an alternative future for the platform. It is speculation that is based on the features of the hardware (i.e., a cable link port) and intentions (e.g., announced cable that was never released). The case of M.K.'s patch for

Mario's Tennis would not be possible without existing code in the game and provides an alternate past in which, presumably, Nintendo had allocated more time and resources to the Virtual Boy (thus allowing for the GameLink cable to be available at launch and for completion of the multiplayer features in *Mario's Tennis*). The *Hyper Fighting* example is slightly different since there is no knowledge that Capcom intended to release a game in the *Street Fighter* series for the Virtual Boy. It paints a plausible alternate past where Capcom signed up for, and was actually developing games for, the Virtual Boy.[5]

With thirty-four announced-and-then-canceled titles (*Planet Virtual Boy* n.d.), it is possible that the Virtual Boy is the only platform for which there are more known canceled than released games. Many of the Virtual Boy's canceled titles had only been announced, with little design or development work. However, there were several games that were ready, or almost ready, for release with rumors of collectors having possession of cartridges and prototypes. So far, two of these have been located and released: *Faceball* (aka Niko-Chan Battle), a game where you "move around and shoot bullets within a 3-D maze as a ball with a smiling face" (*Family Computer Magazine* 1995), and *Bound High!*, a top-down view platformer in development by Japan System Supply where players control a sphere that bounces down (away from the player's view) and "knocks enemies off when it bounces on them" and causes blocks to vanish or "reveal hidden puzzles, items or other objects" (*Nintendo Power* 1996a).

The stories behind the fan releases of both games are long and convoluted. What they share in common is lots of hard work undertaken by fans to get both games to playable states that hopefully reflect their creator's original vision and intention. *Faceball*, in development by Bullet-Proof Software, was first made available as an "80% complete prototype" (Kr155e 2013a). A few months later, *Planet Virtual Boy* user Thunderstruck released *Faceball: Remastered*, which expanded and improved on the prototype by adding a significant number of new levels, enabling features that were originally disabled, and fixing issues with the prototype (Kr155e 2013b). *Bound High!*, presumed to be complete and ready for manufacture (Griffiths 2016), was originally made available after fans obtained a copy of the game's original source code and used it to create a working ROM of the game (Kr155e 2010).[6] Both games also saw eventual limited releases as physical cartridges with custom printed boxes and labels.

Both *Faceball* and *Bound High!* are examples of fans completing the Virtual Boy's softography with titles that could have been "killer apps" for the platform. Both were canceled shortly before they were due for release and would have been part of a second wave of titles for the Virtual Boy. "Bound High contains multiple play modes, which would have made it one of the most fully realized game packages ever produced for Virtual Boy had it shipped" (Parish 2021, 174). It was impressive enough, at the time, that "Nintendo picked it up for release as a first-party title" (Parish 2021, 174). *Faceball* provided a sought-after immersive gameplaying experience in what was then a hot and exciting new game genre: the first-person shooter. As Parish notes, "Faceball would have been the fast-paced FPS the platform truly demanded in the DOOM-obsessed 90s" (Parish 2021, 174). It is, of course, impossible to know if these titles would have, indeed, turned the tide of commercial success for the Virtual Boy. However, it is undeniable that they represent the next step in the platform's alternate future lifecycle—they rounded out the platform's initial set of games.

This is similarly the case for two other highly sought-after canceled games[7]: *Dragon Hopper* and *Zero Racers*. The former, in development by Intelligent Systems, would have been an action-adventure game played from an overhead view in which the player controlled a jumping dragon called Dorin "as he seeks the help of fairies" in rescuing his royal family and his love Diana from the clutches of the "King's power hungry prime minister" (Nintendo 1996). The game's view would "provid[e] a dramatic effect when jumping between multiple levels" as "Dorin is able to leap amazingly high to reach platforms suspended in mid-air, or drop down to hidden areas of stages that appear through holes or at the ends of paths" (Nintendo 1996). *Dragon Hopper*'s place in the platform's softography was akin to a Zelda-like action-adventure game. *Zero Racers*, on the other hand, was to be the platform's first racing game—a fast and futuristic racer that was to be a sequel of sorts to *F-Zero* released on the Super Nintendo. Unlike other games in the series, *Zero Racers*'s racing took place in three dimensions with players racing inside tunnels where they could dive and climb in addition to turning left or right (*Nintendo Power* 1996b).

The research and media archaeological efforts made toward finding, preserving, reconstructing, and eventually releasing canceled games is not unique to the Virtual Boy as a platform. What is special though is the context in which they happen—they reflect a desire to consider and think about the "what if" situations in which the games were released, to play with their potential success, and to consider a present time in which the Virtual Boy, while possibly an oddity, was not seen as a commercial failure but rather as a new branch in the evolutionary tree of game experiences.

Perceptions of the Virtual Boy's Present

A lot has happened in the years since the Virtual Boy's release and cancellation. In the half-decade since it was canceled, the Virtual Boy transitioned

All hail the Virtual Boy!

8.1 A *Tomodachi Life* direct presentation screengrab (Nintendo3DSuk 2014, 2:10).

from being maligned as a commercial failure to being forgotten and ignored. After that, it took on a new role as a cautionary tale for the gaming media (see chapter 7). And for Nintendo, it slowly began to take on a new role as well: a quirky part of Nintendo's history that is referenced in games, with a wink and a smile, for Nintendo's savvy fans to notice and enjoy. The Virtual Boy now sometimes appears in the background of other Nintendo games, for example in the room where players see the trophies they've earned in *Super Smash Bros. Melee* (HAL Laboratory 2001) or next to the television set that appears in the background of the stage named "Gamer" in *Super Smash Bros. for Wii U* (Sora Ltd. and Bandai Namco 2014). It is also often sometimes an in-game collectible item such as in *WarioWare Gold* (Intelligent Systems and Nintendo EPD 2018) or in *Animal Crossing: New Leaf* (Nintendo EAD 2013), where it is available as a furniture item for players to decorate their homes. In *Nintendo Labo VR Kit*, a cardboard "fold-it-yourself" kit designed to, when paired with a Nintendo Switch, function as a pair of virtual reality googles, the Virtual Boy appears "in the flesh" so to speak. *Nintendo Labo VR Kit* has a video section that includes a short clip of gameplay from *Mario's Tennis*. The footage from *Mario's Tennis* is preceded by a title card that says "Virtual Boy: Check out old VR in new VR!" before cutting to a first-person perspective real-world view of a Virtual Boy on a table that is turned around and switched on before the camera zooms in and the view transitions to the Virtual Boy footage (Nintendo 2019).

There are also Virtual Boy appearances that are more humorous. For example, figure 8.1 shows a screenshot from a special video presentation for the Nintendo 3DS title *Tomodachi Life* that featured several famous Nintendo employees portrayed as virtual cartoon (Mii) characters dancing around a Virtual Boy with the caption "All hail the Virtual Boy!" (Nintendo3DSuk 2014). The platform has also been used as a self-deprecating joke. Early in *Luigi's Mansion 3*, "Professor E. Gadd gives Luigi a way to communicate with him as he trawls the many floors of the hotel. It's his latest invention . . . the Virtual Boo" (Next Level Games 2019). The device is described by Professor E. Gadd as a "state-of-the-art virtual reality device" that is "really cutting-edge stuff" and he predicts it will "fly off the shelves" as soon as he finishes "the marketing materials" for it (Next Level Games [2019], as seen in screenshots used in Kohler [2019]).

It is perhaps no surprise that Nintendo's former reluctance to talk about the Virtual Boy seems to have changed. This greater openness also coincides with the resurgent interest in VR. In 2010, stereoscopic 3D television sets started to become widely available (they've since largely disappeared), and 2011 saw the release of Nintendo's 3DS console—a handheld that features stereoscopic 3D effects without the need to look into or wear anything. Approximately a year later, Oculus literally and metaphorically kickstarted a new wave of consumer virtual reality technology, which has since seen growth and diversity with video game companies releasing their own hardware (e.g., Sony's PSVR, Valve's HTC Vive, and the later Valve Index) as well as mainstream VR games.

It is somewhat ironic that the Virtual Boy is sort of cool again because it is misperceived as an early home VR device. One of the reasons for its demise is now the source of its credibility. Of all the historical, pre-Oculus VR systems and devices available for use in the home or arcade, none is more present in the public's imagination and knowledge than the Virtual Boy. The "Virtual" part baked into its name will likely always keep it at the forefront of this historical misperception.

As we have shown, the perception of a platform can sometimes matter more than what it actually does, how it works, and what games were released for it. Furthermore, perceptions of a platform are fluid—shifting and changing as the cultural, technological, and social contexts in which they are used or referred to adjust. We do not know how people will perceive the Virtual Boy in the future. But we do know that it will change—perhaps because Nintendo may rerelease its Virtual Boy games, perhaps because entrepreneurial fans may develop a truly innovative and special Virtual Boy game, or maybe because, partly thanks to this book, it will be explored in even greater depth (pun intended).

Appendix A: Virtual Boy Technical Specifications

CPU—20 MHz 32-bit RISC CPU based on a 32-bit NEC V810 core with customizations. External data bus is 16 bits wide.

Graphics—20 MHz custom virtual image processor (VIP)

Display—Two 384×224-pixel wide-screen displays, one for each eye. Each display is created by a scanned linear array of red LEDs 224 pixels tall by one pixel wide that "draws" the display by sweeping from left to right.

Sound—Custom sound chip (VSU). The VSU includes six channels: four channels for "normal" sound sources with an envelope function; one channel for sound with sweep, modulation, and envelope; and one for noise. Each sound channel draws from data stored in internal wave RAM with a capacity of 6 bits by 32 words for five channels (this excludes the noise channel). The chip can independently control the volume of the left and right stereo output channels. The Virtual Boy has two speakers (for stereo sound) on the left and right of the main unit, a dial for adjusting the volume, and a standard headphone jack.

RAM

- Video RAM (VRM): One megabit of "Dual port" video RAM for displaying images.
- Dynamic RAM (DRAM): One megabit of RAM that stores background data and whatever else the program needs.
- Working RAM (WRAM): 512 kilobits of "pseudo-SRAM," which is used as working memory for the CPU.

ROM—Cartridges can contain up to 128 megabits of ROM and/or RAM.

Power Supply—Six AAA batteries or AC power adaptor (sold separately).

Weight—760 g.

Controller—"M"-shaped controller with a symmetrical buttons placement consisting of two cross-shaped directional pads, one positioned under a thumb on each hand, four circular-shaped face buttons (Select and Start on the left; B and A buttons on the right), and two trigger buttons (L and R) positioned under the index fingers of the left and right hands. The front face of the controller contains the master power switch that powers the Virtual Boy system on and off, and a bulky rectangular detachable battery pack is centered on the posterior.

Dimensions—8.5"×10"×4.3".

Appendix B: Virtual Boy's Games

Over its roughly thirteen months on the market, publishers released twenty-two officially licensed games for the Virtual Boy, fourteen of which came to North America. Of these, eight were Japan-exclusive games, and three were North American exclusives. North American releases were primarily distributed in the United States and Canada, and to a limited extent Mexico and Brazil.

At launch in Japan (July 21, 1995), the Virtual Boy library consisted of five titles: *Mario's Tennis*, *Galactic Pinball*, *Teleroboxer*, *Panic Bomber*, and *Red Alarm*. In North America (August 14, 1995), the launch titles were *Mario's Tennis* (as a pack-in with the system), *Galactic Pinball*, *Teleroboxer*, and *Red Alarm*.

What follows is a list of every officially licensed Virtual Boy game that includes information on each game's international title, developer, publisher, release date, and a brief description.

NA = North American Release
J = Japanese Release

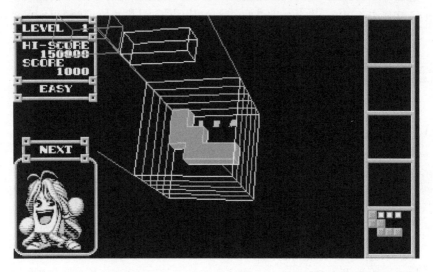

Developer: T&E Soft

Publisher: Nintendo

Released: March 22, 1996 (NA), unreleased in Japan

3D Tetris takes the popular Game Boy killer app into the third dimension by letting players drop 3D polygonal pieces down a shaft shaped like a rectangular prism. The goal is similar to traditional 2D *Tetris*: Fill in a complete layer one block tall to make the layer disappear and score points. It is similar to Alexey Pajitnov's *Welltris* (1989), a sequel of sorts to his original *Tetris*. However, in *Welltris*, the pieces are flat and "fall" down each of the shaft's four walls onto the flat bottom. As in *Tetris*, lines must be made that disappear when completed. Otherwise, *3D Tetris* is perhaps most similar to the 1989 PC game called *Blockout* where the pieces are solid 3D objects (with length, width, and height) in which the player must complete layers. *3D Tetris* has three modes: Center-Fill, 3D Tetris, and Puzzle. It is one of two Virtual Boy games with polygonal wireframe graphics along with *Red Alarm*.

Galactic Pinball

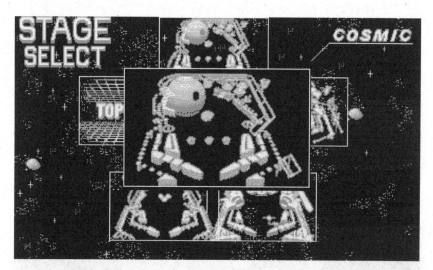

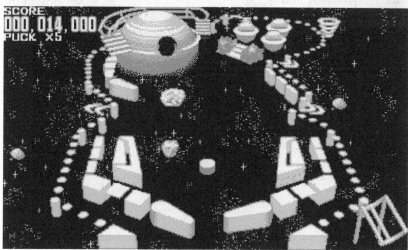

Developer: Intelligent Systems
Publisher: Nintendo
Released: July 21, 1995 (J), August 14, 1995 (NA)

Galactic Pinball was based on the earliest known Virtual Boy game prototype *Space Pinball*, which Nintendo showed to the press in early demos. Gunpei Yokoi thought pinball set in space would be enveloping because the Virtual Boy display's ability to show absolute blackness suggests infinite space behind the "table."

The game features four tables: Cosmic, Colony, UFO, and Alien—all played like a traditional pinball game with two flippers, although there are also special bonus areas. The Cosmic table features a notable bonus mode that includes a controllable version of Samus Aran's Gunship (from the *Metroid* series) where players shoot enemies from Metroid in a short minigame.

Golf (NA) / T&E Virtual Golf (J)

Developer: T&E Soft

Publisher: Nintendo (NA), T&E Soft (J)

Released: November 1, 1995 (NA), November 8, 1995 (J)

Golf is a realistic golf simulation in the vein of PC titles like *Links: The Challenge of Golf* (1990). While setting up your shot, you can choose your direction, club, and stance. Hitting the ball involves precise timing on a power meter and on a slice/spin display of a digitized golf ball. While taking a shot, you see an animated digitized human golfer standing on 3D polygonal terrain, and the ball moves and rolls accordingly. Trees are 2D sprites.

Unlike golf games on other platforms, you can see the depth of the terrain as your ball rolls away from you, which adds a lot to the experience over conventional 2D titles.

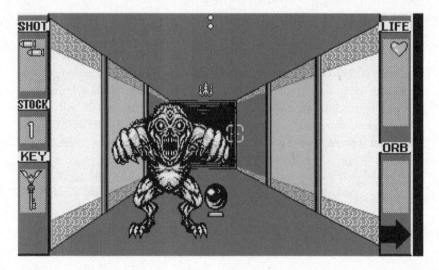

Developer: Be Top

Publisher: I'Max

Released: October 13, 1995 (J), unreleased in North America

In *Innsmouse No Yakata*—inspired by the 1931 H. P. Lovecraft novella *The Shadow over Innsmouth*—you enter a haunted mansion, seeking two mapping orbs and a key to the exit in each stage. Among the small Virtual Boy catalog, this title is notable for its full thematic embrace of horror, unlike the other mostly kid-friendly games on the platform. It's a stressful, atmospheric corridor action title with forty-five stages and multiple endings.

Innsmouse plays like a 1980s maze game but with a first-person perspective looking down the halls of the mansion as you move around. It adds a controllable crosshair for shooting monsters (controlled with the right D-pad) and the need to reload your limited shots with the left trigger button. In that sense, it's almost a first-person shooter, but with few bullets available and slow crosshair movement, the shooting aspect is awkward, and the player ends up running away as much as engaging with the H. R. Giger–like enemies. You're also fighting a timer on each stage, which runs down quickly. And while a true FPS like *Wolfenstein 3D* port may have worked well on this system, *Innsmouse* is as close as the Virtual Boy got in a licensed release.

Jack Bros. (NA) / Jack Bros. no Airo de Hiihoo (J)

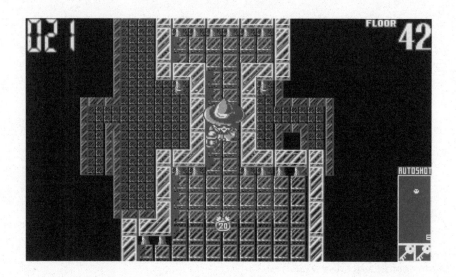

Developer: Atlus

Publisher: Atlus

Released: September 29, 1995 (J), October 20, 1995 (NA)

In *Jack Bros.*, you can choose to play as Jack Frost, Jack Lantern, or Jack Skelton. In the story, it's October 31—Halloween—the one day of the year when fairies can enter the human world. Jack stays too long and is in danger of losing his powers if he doesn't make it home. To get home, you'll travel through six different fantasy worlds that consist of maze-like levels seen from an overhead (birds-eye view) perspective. As you play, you can see the next floor in the background below the current floor on a different depth layer.

To progress, you need to collect all the keys on each floor to unlock the exit. Along the way, you'll find increasingly difficult monsters to kill and hazards to negotiate. Once you unlock the exit, you jump down to the next floor below. *Jack Bros.* partially feels like a twin-stick shooter (without the sticks). It makes good use of the two D-pads on the VB controller: The left pad moves your character, and the right pad attacks in the direction you press. *Jack Bros.* is a spin-off of the *Megami Tensei* series (the first to see release outside Japan), and it's usually regarded as one of the best games on the Virtual Boy.

Mario Clash

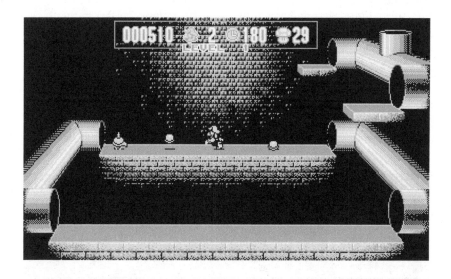

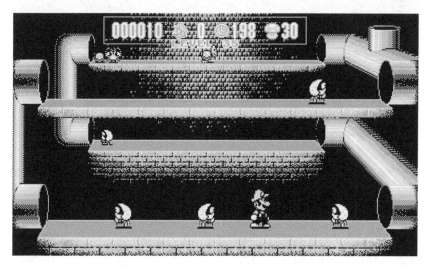

Developer: Nintendo R&D1

Publisher: Nintendo

Released: September 28, 1995 (J), October 1, 1995 (NA)

Mario Clash takes place in an impossibly tall and narrow forty-story tower ("Clash Tower") that stretches upward through the clouds. All forty levels are selectable at the start of the game, and the goal of each is to clear all of the increasingly difficult enemies by stomping on koopas and tossing their shells.

Mario Clash is arguably a spin-off of *Mario Bros.* (1983) but with the added element of gameplay at different stereoscopic depths. Unlike its precursor, in *Mario Clash*, Mario can travel in the foreground or background by passing through pipes, and also on an upper or lower level in each depth layer. Mario can also toss koopas between the foreground and background, adding extra complexity to the game.

Mario's Tennis

Developer: Nintendo R&D1

Publisher: Nintendo

Released: July 21, 1995 (J), August 14, 1995 (NA)

While we're now familiar with living in a world full of *Mario Golf*, *Mario Sluggers*, *Mario Strikers*, and so on, *Mario's Tennis* was the first-ever game to tie the Mario cast into a traditional sports game with a *Mario* title. It's a fairly traditional tennis game: you can play Singles or Doubles against a computer player in a single game or tournament with minimal options. Unlike, say, *Mario Kart*, there are no power-ups or wild Mushroom Kingdom items to spice up gameplay. It's just a regular tennis game with Mario, Luigi, Princess Peach, Yoshi, Toad, Koopa, and Donkey Kong Jr. As a result, the game can get stale quickly.

Notably, *Mario's Tennis* was the pack-in game for the US launch of the Virtual Boy, and it serves as an introduction to the depth effects on the system. It also utilizes a "Mode 7"–like scaling technique to display a flat tennis court bitmap in three dimensions.

In August of 2017, a PlanetVB user by the name M.K. announced that they had found unused multiplayer code in *Mario's Tennis* and were able to restore two of the three multiplayer game modes via a patch for the game. Players are currently able to play multiplayer matches via the use of a fan-created link cable (a product that Nintendo announced but never released) finally making good on the promise in an early promotional video that mentions the possibility of two-player gameplay.

Developer: Nintendo R&D3, Saffire

Publisher: Nintendo (NA)

Released: February 26, 1996 (NA), unreleased in Japan

This American-only release features a unique starring role for *Nintendo Power* magazine's former cartoon mascot, Nester, who featured in "Howard & Nester" and then "Nester's Adventures" comic strips between 1988 and

1993. In the game, we also meet "Hester" for the first time, who is Nester's sister.

Aside from the Nester elements, *Nester's Funky Bowling* is a competent bowling simulator that focuses mostly on a realistic portrayal of the sport. It has three modes: Bowl, Practice, and Challenge (where you attempt to knock down novel arrangements of pins), and it can be played with one player or two players alternating at the same console. *Funky Bowling* also features detailed animations of Nester reacting to how many pins he knocks down. As one of the final games released for the Virtual Boy, it's also fairly rare.

Panic Bomber (NA) / Tobidase! Panibomb (J)

Developer: Eighting, Hudson Soft

Publisher: Nintendo (NA), Hudson Soft (J)

Released: July 21, 1995 (J), December 1, 1995 (NA)

Panic Bomber originated on the PC Engine in 1994 and later received ports for quite a few systems, including the Virtual Boy. As a result, this falling-block puzzle game is one of a handful of Virtual Boy games whose gameplay does not benefit much from the depth capabilities of the platform. This version also lacks color for differentiating the block types. Depth effects are limited to cosmetic flourishes like layered menus that have no effect on gameplay.

    Panic Bomber borrows from *Puyo Puyo*, but with Bomberman characters and graphical elements grafted on. To play, you rotate groups of three blocks and drop them into a play area. When three of the same block type line up, they disappear, replaced by bombs. When a lit bomb drops, it can ignite the other bombs, causing a chain reaction for a higher score. Meanwhile, you're playing against a computer-controlled player, attempting to cause them to fail. Gameplay ends when the blocks reach the top of the screen.

Red Alarm

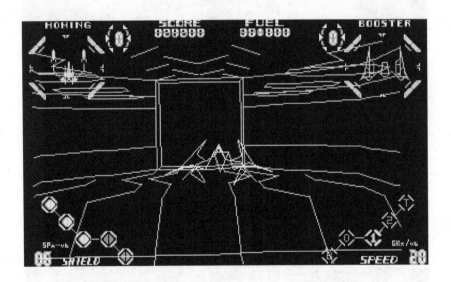

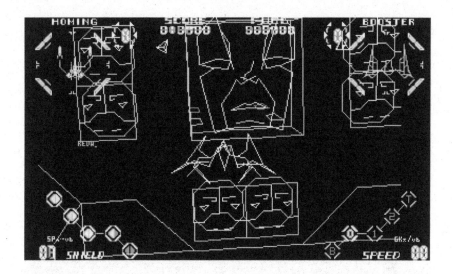

Developer: T&E Soft

Publisher: Nintendo (NA), T&E Soft (J)

Released: July 21, 1995 (J), August 14, 1995 (NA)

In *Red Alarm*, you control a Tech-Wing space fighter in a quest to defeat KAOS over the course of six levels with a boss fight at the end of each one. It's an immersive, behind-the-ship shoot-'em-up similar to *Star Fox* where you're generally moving forward while controlling your ship's speed, maneuvering, and shooting enemies. Notably, the right D-pad is used to quickly "dash" your ship up, down, left, or right for dodging incoming fire.

Red Alarm is unique on the Virtual Boy for being the only 3D polygonal action combat game (*3D Tetris* uses 3D polygons too, and *Golf* uses some for the terrain). Instead of stacking flat layers for a diorama effect, it uses its own 3D engine to draw wireframe polygonal graphics, which really pop in stereoscopic 3D. But with no flat shading or texture mapping, the visuals can become slightly confusing at times since you can see right through the 3D objects. It's one of the most notable and distinctive games on the system.

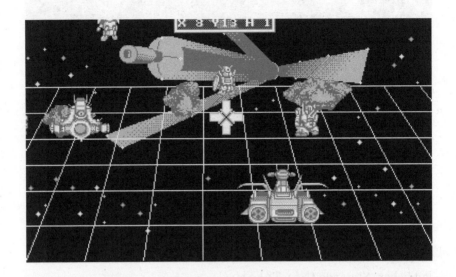

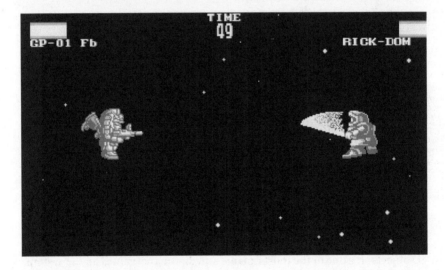

Developer: Locomotive Corporation

Publisher: Bandai (J)

Released: December 22, 1995 (J), unreleased in North America

SD Gundam Dimension War is a turn-based strategy game set in space with action combat sequences. It's based on the popular *Gundam* anime series in Japan, and it was the Virtual Boy's final Japanese game release along with

Virtual Bowling. During the turn-based portion of the game, you see a map with mechs and ships positioned against a star field and among asteroids. You can move units along a grid and attack enemy units.

The action combat sequences involve two phases: a) an approach, where you shoot at the enemy as it draws near, and b) an all-out one-on-one combat screen. During both phases, depth plays a role, but more so in the second phase where you can position your warrior or ship within three distinct depth planes from foreground to background while shooting various weapons. The ultimate goal is to destroy the enemy's battle cruisers to progress to the next level. Despite its unique genre for the platform, critics generally consider it an unremarkable game.

Space Invaders: Virtual Collection

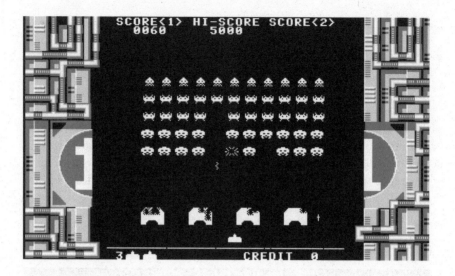

Developer: Taito

Publisher: Taito (J)

Released: December 1, 1995 (J), unreleased in North America

This rare Japanese-only release combines two classic arcade games, *Space Invaders* (1978) and *Space Invaders Part II* (1979), into a unique presentation on the Virtual Boy. You can play either game in its original 2D arcade version (entirely 2D, no depth) or in a special "Virtual 3D" mode that tilts the playfield backward in space and shows the rows of space aliens with depth—sort of like a carnival shooting duck gallery.

Virtual Collection also includes a "Challenge" mode, which is similar to the Virtual 3D mode but you can pick "Time Attack" or "Score Attack" and try to top your previous records.

Space Squash

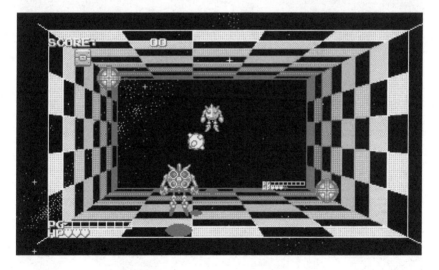

Developer: Tomcat System

Publisher: Coconuts Japan Entertainment (J)

Released: September 28, 1995 (J), unreleased in North America

In *Space Squash*, you play as a robot pitted against a similar robotic opponent in a futurist sport that resembles a type of 3D *Pong* (if you imagine taking the perspective just behind the paddle looking forward at an opponent). You can move your robot up, down, left, or right, and you attempt to swat the ball back by pressing up, left, or right on the right D-pad. If you miss the ball and it gets past you, your opponent scores a point.

Unlike the real game of squash, you're not taking turns bouncing the ball against a wall, but the "court" does have four walls that the ball can bounce off of, similar to the walls in *Pong*, but in three dimensions. Power-ups along the way spice things up, and it has a training mode as well. It makes extensive use of the depth features of the Virtual Boy.

Teleroboxer

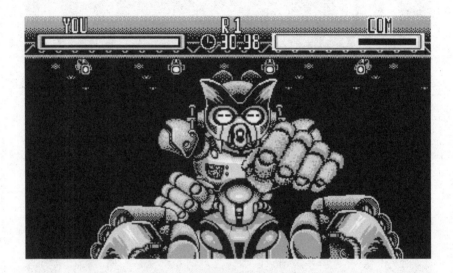

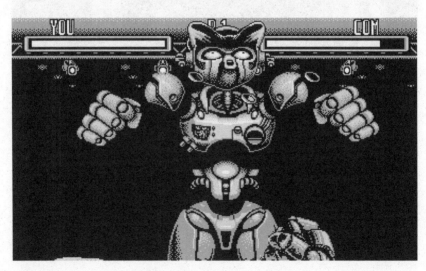

Developer: Nintendo R&D1, Nintendo R&D3

Publisher: Nintendo

Released: July 21, 1995 (J), August 14, 1995 (NA)

Teleroboxer is an immersive first-person boxing simulator where you pilot a giant robot fighting against other humans piloting giant robots. As illustrated in the game's introduction, your in-game character wears a visor (like you, peering into the Virtual Boy) controlling the robot's fists. You control your robot's left and right fists independently: the left D-pad and left trigger button handle the left fist, and the right D-Pad and trigger operate the right fist. Each D-pad sets the type of punch (high, low, side, uppercut), and the trigger button executes the punch. You can also guard and dodge.

Notably, the opponent robots are made up of separate sprite pieces that move independently, scaling, moving, and rotating relative to each other to animate the character. With only seven opponents total, *Teleroboxer* is fairly light on content, but its game style makes it a unique title on the platform.

V-Tetris

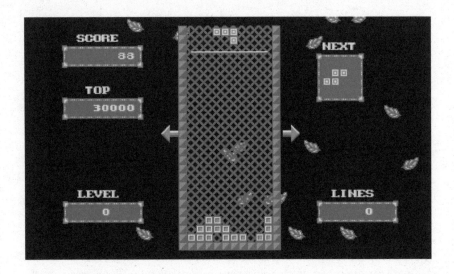

Developer: Locomotive Corporation

Publisher: Bullet-Proof Software (J)

Released: August 25, 1995 (J), unreleased in North America

Unlike *3D Tetris*, *V-Tetris* is mostly a vanilla 2D *Tetris* experience. Game mode A is like a typical *Tetris* game: you play for as long as possible, trying to get a record-high score or number of lines cleared. In mode B, you try to make as many points as possible while clearing twenty-five lines. Both game types recall the A and B modes in the Nintendo's Game Boy version of *Tetris* (1989). The Virtual Boy's depth capabilities play no part in modes A and B.

Where *V-Tetris* diverges from the standard Tetris formula is with game mode C, which allows you to virtually "rotate" the column of deposited tetrominos left and right (with the Left and Right trigger buttons) until you make lines. As you rotate them, you'll see certain pieces move into the background "behind" the active game play area and on a different depth layer. It does not require depth to play, so *V-Tetris* is a 2D game with cosmetic 3D depth elements tacked on.

Vertical Force

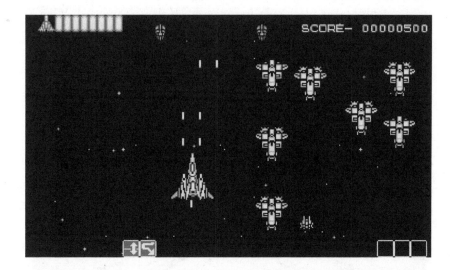

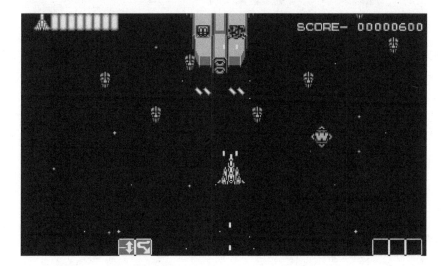

Developer: Hudson Soft

Publisher: Nintendo (NA), Hudson Soft (J)

Released: August 12, 1995 (J), December 1, 1995 (NA)

Vertical Force is notable for being the only "shmup" (shoot-'em-up) on the Virtual Boy in the vein of *Blazing Lazers* or *Star Soldier*. It's a vertical-scrolling space shooter where you control a starship called *Ragnarok* in a battle to defend Earth. On the way, you'll collect power-ups (wide shot, laser, shield, bombs) and AI Drones to help you.

Gameplay takes place over five stages, which isn't unusual. What is unusual is that it also takes place on two depth planes: foreground or background, and you can switch between them at any time, using them to dodge enemies or shoot enemies on either plane.

Virtual Bowling

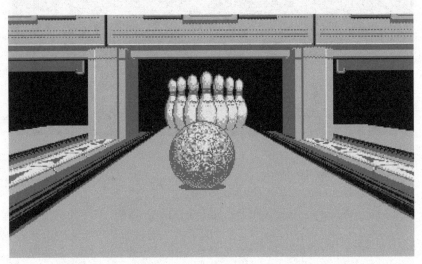

Developer: Athena

Publisher: Athena (J)

Released: December 22, 1995 (J), unreleased in North America

Virtual Bowling feels like a sophisticated realistic bowling simulator, taking into account bowler position, aim, spin, and power. You can also specify the weight of your bowling ball and how much of the bowling lane is waxed. The game plays it straight with no whimsical flourishes, and you can pick Standard, Tournament, and Training modes.

As you roll your ball in *Virtual Bowling*, you get a special visual treat: a first-person camera view just behind the bowling ball as it rolls down the lane and hits the pins. If you get a strike, you see a special animation. It's quite dramatic in 3D.

Virtual Boy Wario Land (NA) / Virtual Boy Wario Land: Awazon no Hihou (J)

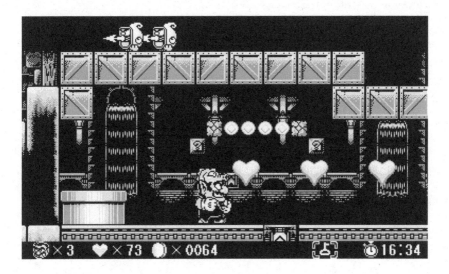

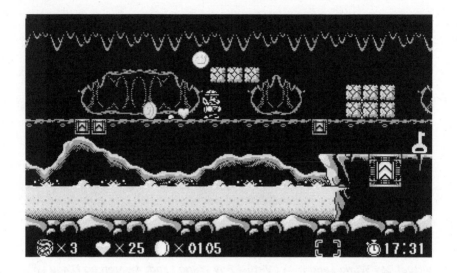

Developer: Nintendo R&D1

Publisher: Nintendo

Released: December 1, 1995 (J), November 27, 1995 (NA)

Of all the games on the Virtual Boy, *Wario Land* is generally regarded as the most polished and complete. It's a side-scrolling platformer that will be familiar to any fan of the *Mario* or *Wario Land* game series. It contains fourteen levels, two mini games, four power-up forms, and lots of secrets. Two of the power-ups result from combining other power-ups. In every level, you need to find a key to escape, and you get bonus points for discovering hidden treasures.

Virtual Boy Wario Land delivers on the console's depth capabilities with pseudo-3D objects as well as dioramic layering effects of sprites. In particular, gameplay can take place in the foreground or background on two different depth layers, which Wario can jump between using special pads.

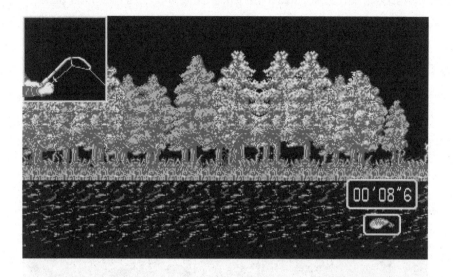

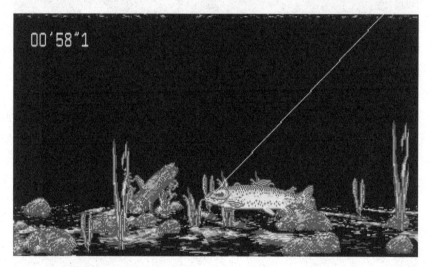

Developer: Locomotive Corporation

Publisher: Pack-In-Video (J)

Released: October 6, 1995 (J), unreleased in North America

Virtual Fishing is a basic fishing simulator game that approaches realism
to some degree. In one mode, you try to catch the longest fish possible,

and in another you try to catch as many fish as you can within a time limit. You can also participate in a fishing tournament against computer players.

While casting your line, you see a view of the water going back into the distance. When the fish bites (and your hook sets), the view switches to a side view underwater where the fish on the line swims among various plant life. Overall, the stereoscopic depth gives it some graphical flair but doesn't affect gameplay.

Virtual Lab

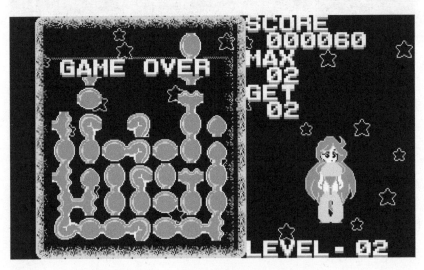

Developer: Nacoty

Publisher: J-Wing (J)

Released: December 8, 1995 (J), unreleased in North America

Virtual Lab is probably the most bizarre licensed Virtual Boy release. It's a bare bones falling block puzzle game (a genre originally defined by *Tetris*) with lackluster graphics and no options other than three game speeds. Your goal is to complete tracts of organic tubing (that look like pulsating intestines) using various segments that you can rotate while dropping in place.

Perhaps to make up for the very basic graphics that don't utilize stereoscopic features at all, *Virtual Lab* features a long-haired anime-style girl on the right side of the screen who dances (with jiggling stereoscopic anatomy, it must be noted), with no apparent reason for being there other than distracting eye candy.

Virtual League Baseball (NA) / _Virtual Pro Yakyuu '95_ (J)

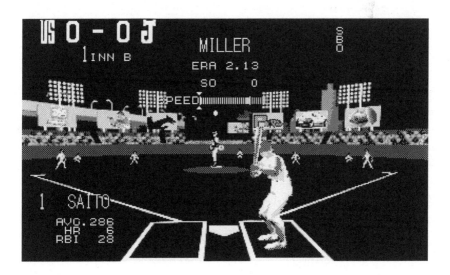

Developer: Kemco

Publisher: Kemco

Released: August 11, 1995 (J), September 11, 1995 (NA)

In this baseball game, you play as one of twenty-three baseball teams (which differ between American and Japanese versions of the game) in a single match, all-star game, or pennant race. In general, it looks like a typical video game baseball simulation from the late 1980s or early 1990s in the way it handles being at bat, pitching, and manning the field.

In the Japanese version of the game (*Virtual Pro Yakyuu '95*), the players are represented by large "chibi" characters with cartoonish, childlike proportions. In the North American version, the players have the more "realistic" appearance of regularly proportioned adult humans. Either way, the graphics are grainy and lack sharp detail, but the addition of perceiving the depth of the approaching ball while batting is a novelty.

Waterworld

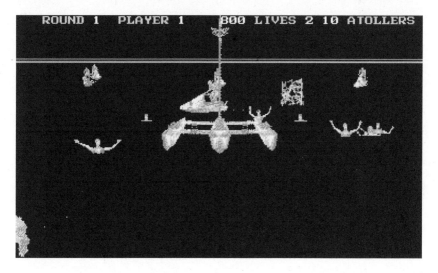

Developer: Ocean Software

Publisher: Ocean of America (NA)

Released: December 21, 1995 (NA), unreleased in Japan

This unusual American-only release is a licensed title for the 1995 post-apocalyptic action film of the same name starring Kevin Costner. It feels like a version of *Asteroids* with a third-person, over-the-shoulder viewpoint set in the ocean. You play as a boat that can shoot unlimited times out of its bow, and you can rotate your ship in any direction and move forward. You can also zoom out with dynamic scaling effects that appear unique for games at the time.

In structure, *Waterworld* borrows a lot from 1980s arcade games like *Defender*. During each round of play, you must destroy a certain number of enemies ("smokers") riding personal watercraft. Meanwhile, those enemies attempt to abduct your friends ("atollers") and carry them away. You get a bonus at the end of every round for each atoller still alive in the "water" (which is completely black).

Notes

Chapter 1

1. Wittenhagen's coverage even includes author Zagal's own (mediocre) *Channel Sweeper* game, which was designed and developed in a few hours in the context of the 2010 Global Game Jam.

Chapter 2

1. 3D Pole Position was listed on the 3D Imager's packaging but never released commercially.

Chapter 3

1. In October 1995, this would have been approximately US$388, more than double its price in the United States (https://tradingeconomics.com/brazil/currency).
2. After thirty-one years working at Nintendo, he left on August 15, 1996, to pursue other opportunities. It was widely, and incorrectly, believed at the time that this was due to the Virtual Boy's failure.

Chapter 4

1. Some CRTs would alternate between even- and odd-numbered horizontal lines—first "drawing" all the odd-numbered lines and then the even ones.
2. For OBJs, if the parallax attribute is a positive integer, this will result in an uncrossed disparity and objects will appear closer than the Virtual Screen (the left image is displaced to the right, and the right image is displaced to the left). The opposite happens when the parallax attributed is a negative integer (the left image is displaced to the left, and the right image is displaced to the right). The origin ($X=0$) is the top-left corner of the display.

Chapter 5

1. A notable exception is 3dSenVR, an NES emulator that "that converts classic and homebrew NES games into full 3D experiences in realtime and let you play them in VR" (Geodstudio 2019) in a way that "effectively turns [supported games] into playable dioramas" (Grabarczyk 2020).
2. https://www.flickr.com/photos/hopkinsarchives/4683026952/in/photostream/ and https://www.flickr.com/photos/hopkinsarchives/4682397665/in/photostream/.
3. Visually, the character stays in the same spot in the center-bottom of the screen, and the court and opponent move around.

Chapter 6

1. In Europe, the tagline was "Sega does what Nintendon't." The difference in taglines was probably because the Genesis was sold as the Mega Drive outside of North America.
2. As a buzzword, it even made its way into audio—as "3D audio" or surround sound. The first computer soundcard to support 3D audio was the Diamond Monster Sound card released in 1997 (Collins 2008, 64).
3. Notable earlier attempts were sold as peripherals or add-ons to existing devices even when they provided significant additional processing and technical capabilities such as the Sega CD for the Sega Genesis (1992) and the TurboGrafx-CD/CD-ROM² for the TurboGrafx (1988).
4. To be fair, the materiality of console games had been complicated earlier. For example, Nintendo's own Famicom Disk System peripheral, officially released only in Japan in 1986, used a proprietary floppy disk format, thus blurring the lines with home computers.
5. 3DO's model did not ultimately succeed partly because to create momentum in the market the hardware should be priced below cost—and 3DO's hardware licensors were not willing to do that (Brandenburger and Nalebuff 1995).
6. An additional complicating factor was the experimentation at the time with console add-ons, the most notable being the Sega CD (see endnote 3 in this chapter) and the Sega 32X both for the Sega Genesis. The Sega 32X, released in 1994, was an add-on designed as a stopgap to extend the Sega Genesis's market lifespan prior to the release of the Sega Saturn. It was not a commercial success.

Chapter 7

1. Famously, Sony removed the rumble feature from its Sixaxis controller that was bundled with its PlayStation 3 controller only to quickly reintroduce it (after public outcry) with the DualShock 3 controller that became standard for the platform.
2. Released as *Siren* in the United States and Japan.
3. Dark objects that are far away tend to look more blue because blue light is scattered more by moisture and dust in the atmosphere (e.g., mountains) (Britannica Editors 1999).

Chapter 8

1. See https://shmuplations.com/yokoixeno/ for Alexander Highsmith's English translation of Yokoi's interview in Eno (1996).
2. Coauthor Benj Edwards created the BX Foundry BX-240 and BX-250, which were produced in limited numbers in late 2018 and early 2019.
3. None of the commercially released games made use of the cable either.
4. *Planet Virtual Boy* (www.planetvb.com) is widely considered the largest and most influential Virtual Boy fan site (Mora-Cantallops and Bergillos 2018). Most of the community's activity now resides on a Discord server, but the site continues to be the most comprehensive repository for Virtual Boy information—both present and past.
5. None of the currently known canceled commercial Virtual Boy games were being developed by Capcom.
6. *Bound High!* was rereleased eight years later when a prototype cartridge was obtained and dumped. There are no visible differences between the cartridge-dumped version and the one created from source code.
7. This footnote is just to indicate that, going by Murphy's Law, the fan community will have located prototypes of these games, thus rendering this book obsolete by the time it sees print.

References

Altice, Nathan. 2015. *I Am Error: The Nintendo Family Computer/Entertainment System Platform*. Platform Studies. Cambridge, MA: MIT Press.

Anderson, John. 1983. "Who Really Invented the Video Game?" *Creative Computing Video & Arcade Games* 1, no. 1(Spring): 8–11. https://ia800200.us.archive.org/23/items/Creative_Computing_Video_Arcade_Games_01_spring83/Creative_Computing_Video_Arcade_Games_01_spring83_text.pdf.

Aoyama, Yuko, and Hiro Izushi. 2003. "Hardware Gimmick or Cultural Innovation? Technological, Cultural, and Social Foundations of the Japanese Video Game Industry." *Research Policy* 32: 423–444.

Arsenault, Dominic. 2017. *Super Power, Spoony Bards, and Silverware: The Super Nintendo Entertainment System*. Cambridge, MA: MIT Press.

Arsenault, Dominic, and Audrey Larochelle. 2013. "From Euclidean Space to Albertian Gaze: Traditions of Visual Representation in Games beyond the Surface." In *Proceedings of the 2013 DiGRA Conference: DeFragging Game Studies*. Atlanta: Digital Games Research Association (DiGRA). http://www.digra.org/digital-library/publications/from-euclidean-space-to-albertian-gaze-traditions-of-visual-representation-in-games-beyond-the-surface/.

Arsenault, Dominic, Pierre-Marc Côté, Audrey Larochelle, and Sacha Lebel. 2013. "Graphical Technologies, Innovation and Aesthetics in the Video Game Industry: A Case Study of the Shift from 2D to 3D Graphics in the 1990s." *GAME* 02. https://www.gamejournal.it/wp-content/uploads/2019/08/GAME_02_Technology-Perspective_Journal_Arsenault_Cot%C3%A9_Larochelle_Lebel.pdf.

Asmik. 1991. *D-Force Instruction Booklet*. Asmik Corporation.

Atlus. 1995. *Jack Bros. Instruction Booklet*. Atlus Software.

Australian GamePro. 2004. "Nintendo's Revolution." August/September 2004, 8.

Balland, Pierre-Alexandre, Mathijs De Vaan, and Ron Boschma. 2013. "The Dynamics of Interfirm Networks along the Industry Life Cycle: The Case of the Global

Video Game Industry, 1987–2007." *Journal of Economic Geography* 13 (5): 741–765. https://doi.org/10.1093/jeg/lbs023.

Barrier, Michael. 1999. *Hollywood Cartoons: American Animation in Its Golden Age*. Oxford and New York: Oxford University Press.

Becker, Allan. 1990. Miniature Video Display System. USPTO US4934773A, filed July 27, 1987, and issued June 19, 1990. https://patents.google.com/patent/US4934773A/en.

Blundell, Barry G. 2008. *An Introduction to Computer Graphics and Creative 3-D Environments*. London: Springer.

Bogost, I., and N. Montfort. 2007. "New Media as Material Constraint: An Introduction to Platform Studies." http://www.bogost.com/downloads/Bogost%20Montfort%20HASTAC.pdf.

Bogost, I., and N. Montfort. 2009. "Platform Studies: Frequently Questioned Answers." https://escholarship.org/content/qt01rok9br/qt01rok9br.pdf.

Boyer, Steven. 2009. "A Virtual Failure: Evaluating the Success of Nintendo's Virtual Boy." *The Velvet Light Trap* 64: 22–23. http://doi.org/10.1353/vlt.0.0039

Bradbury, S. 1967. *The Evolution of the Microscope*. Oxford, UK: Pergamon Press.

Brandenburger, Adam M., and Barry J. Nalebuff. 1995. "The Right Game: Use Game Theory to Shape Strategy." *Harvard Business Review* (July–August): 57–71. https://hbr.org/1995/07/the-right-game-use-game-theory-to-shape-strategy

Brewster, David. 1858. *The Kaleidoscope: Its History, Theory, and Construction with Its Application to the Fine and Useful Arts*. 2nd ed. London: John Murray.

Britannica Editors. 1999. "Aerial Perspective." *Encyclopaedia Britannica*. https://www.britannica.com/art/aerial-perspective.

Burdea, Grigore, and Philippe Coiffet. 2003. *Virtual Reality Technology*. 2nd ed. Hoboken, NJ: John Wiley & Sons.

Burman, Rob. 2004. "Boktai 2: Solar Boy Django." *Nintendo Official Magazine (UK)*, no. 147(December): 65.

Campagnoni, Donata Pesenti, and Nicoletta Pacini, eds. 2016. *National Cinema Musem Turin: The Visitor's Guide*. Milano, Italy: Silvana Editoriale.

Camper, Brett. 2009. "Fake Bit: Imitation and Limitation." In *Proceedings of DAC 2009*. Irvine, CA. https://escholarship.org/uc/item/3s67474h.

Capcom. 1992. *Street Fighter II Turbo: Hyper Fighting*. Super Nintendo Entertainment System (SNES).

Cifaldi, Frank. 2011. "Loose Lips: The Quotable History of Nintendo's Virtual Boy." *GameDeveloper.Com* (blog). https://www.gamedeveloper.com/business/loose-lips-the-quotable-history-of-nintendo-s-virtual-boy.

Clarkson, Mark. 1995. "A Magic Carpet Ride." *Computer Gaming World*, no. 127(February): 122–126.

Collins, Karen. 2008. *Game Sound: An Introduction to the History, Theory, and Practice of Video Game Music and Sound Design*. Cambridge, MA: MIT Press.

Cube. 2004a. "Goblin Commander: Unleash the Horde." no. 28, January 2004, 44–45.

Cube. 2004b. "Hands on with the DS." no. 34, 2004, 32–35.

Cube. 2004c. "Innovate or Die." no. 34, 2004, 14–15.

Custodio, Alex. 2020. *Who Are You? Nintendo's Game Boy Advance Platform*. Cambridge, MA: MIT Press.

Darrigol, Olivier. 2012. *A History of Optics from Greek Antiquity to the Nineteenth Century*. Oxford: Oxford University Press.

Daukantas, Patricia. 2010. "A Short History of Laser Light Shows." *Optics and Photonics News* 21 (5): 42–47.

Delaney, Ben. 2014. *Sex Drugs and Tessellation: The Truth about Virtual Reality*. Oakland, CA: CyberEdge Information Services.

Dettmer, Roger. 2001. "Changing Processors." *IEE Review* 47, 3: 38–40..

Diamond Multimedia. 1995. "Diamond Edge Advertisement: Karate." *Next Generation*.

Dillard, Corbie. 2012. "Interview: Mutant Mudds Reader Question." *NintendoLife* (blog). January 6, 2012. https://web.archive.org/web/20150415092903/http://www.nintendolife.com/news/2012/01/interview_mutant_mudds_reader_questions.

DogP. 2010. "Link Cable Project Interest." *Planet Virtual Boy* (blog). November 11, 2010. https://www.virtual-boy.com/forums/t/link-cable-project-interest/.

Donovan, Tristan. 2010. *Replay: The History of Video Games*. Lewes, United Kingdom: Yellow Ant.

Edge Magazine. 1994. "Argonaut Software." no. 5, February 1994, 24–29.

Edge Magazine. 2021. "Reality Check." no. 358, June 2021, 8–11.

Edwards, Benj. 2014. "Virtual Boy Wasteland." *Vintage Computing and Gaming* (blog). January 13, 2014. https://www.vintagecomputing.com/index.php/archives/1023/retro-scan-of-the-week-virtual-boy-wasteland.

Edwards, Benj. 2015. "Unraveling the Enigma of Nintendo's Virtual Boy, 20 Years Later." *FastCompany* (blog). August 21, 2015. https://www.fastcompany.com/3050016/unraveling-the-enigma-of-nintendos-virtual-boy-20-years-later.

Effie. n.d. "Nintendo—Play It Loud." Accessed February 8, 2018. https://effie.org/case_database/case/NA_1995_300.

Electronic Gaming Monthly. 1995a. "Bull's Eye: Virtual Boy's Special Day Has Gamers Seeing Red." no. 76, November 1995, 22, 24.

Electronic Gaming Monthly. 1995b. "In the Zone." no. 77, December 1995, 26.

Electronic Gaming Monthly. 1995c. "Tidbits . . ." no. 77, December 1995, 26.

Electronic Gaming Monthly. 1997. "Behind the Screens: Shake It Up Baby." no. 95, June 1997, 74.

EGM2. 1995. "Nintendo, NBC and Blockbuster Strutting Their Stuff with Virtual Boy Promo." volume 2, no. 1 (July): 27.

Engler, Craig. 1992. "Affordable VR by 1994." *Computer Gaming World*, 100, 80-81. November 1992.

Engst, Adam. 1990. "Head-Mounted Screen." *TidBits* (blog). April 23, 1990. https://tidbits.com/1990/04/23/head-mounted-screen/.

Eno, Kenji. 1996. "Gunpei Yokoi x Kenji Eno—Developer Interview." In *The Book of Kenji Eno—A Bit of This and That—Game Criticism Special* [飯野賢治の本 ナンだ かイロイロ ゲーム批評　特別編集] (*Game Hihyou, Volume #13*). Translated by Alex Highsmith, 84–88. Japan: Micro Design. .

Esposito, N. 2005. "How Video Game History Shows Us Why Video Game Nostalgia Is So Important Now." Gainesville, FL. http://nicolasesposito.fr/publications_fichiers/esposito2005history.pdf.

Family Computer Magazine Staff. 1995. "3D Virtual Boy Magazine (Supplement)." Translated by Benjamin Stevens. *Family Computer Magazine*, volume 11, no. 10, June 16, 1995.

Fittipaldi, Mário. 1993. "A Nintendo Já Chegou." *Videogame*, volume 3, no. 3, September 1993, 7.

Fitzpatrick, Eileen. 1994. "Nintendo Reverses Stand, Will Play the Rental Game." *Billboard*, April 30, 1994, 6, 97.

Fleckenstein, Kristie S. 2016. "Materiality's Rhetorical Work: The Nineteenth-Century Parlor Stereoscope and the Second-Naturing of Vision." In *Rhetoric, Through Everyday Things*, edited by Scott Barnett and Casey Boyle, 125–138. Tuscaloosa: The University of Alabama Press.

Folhina. 1995. "Herois de filmes e da TV Viram Bonecos." *Folha de Sao Paulo*, September 22, 1995, 6.

Frank, Allegra. 2015. "Miyamoto Reveals the Truth about Bowser Jr., Super Mario 3 Myths." *Polygon* (blog). September 10, 2015. https://www.polygon.com/2015/9/10/9301773/miyamoto-bowser-jr-super-mario-3-myths.

Furness, Thomas. 2014. "Introduction." In *Sex Drugs and Tessellation: The Truth about Virtual Reality as Revealed in the Pages of CyberEdge Journal* edited by Ben Delaney, vii–x. Oakland, CA: CyberEdge Information Services.

Future Staff. 2001. "Kirby's Tilt 'n' Tumble." *Videogames: The Ultimate Guide*.

Gagnon Hawkins, Diana. 1995. "Virtual Reality and Passive Simulators: The Future of Fun." In *Communication in the Age of Virtual Reality*, edited by Frank Biocca and Mark L. Levy, 159–189. Hillsdale, NJ: Lawrence Erlbaum Associates.

Games Staff. 2004a. "Forbidden Siren." *Games (Australia Edition)*, no. 11, 73–75.

Games Staff. 2004b. "Nintendo's Screen Test." *Games (Australia Edition)*, no. 11, 6–7.

Geodstudio. 2019. "Play NES Games in 3D & VR." http://www.geodstudio.net/.

Gillen, Marilyn. 1994. "Sega, Nintendo Bring Plans to CES." *Billboard*, July 9, 1994, 70.

Gillen, Marilyn. 1995. "Video Games Poised for '96, Beyond." *Billboard*, December 23, 1995, 78.

Glazer, Sara. 1991. "Electromagnetic Fields: Are They Dangerous?" *CQ Researcher*, April 26, 1991. https://library.cqpress.com/cqresearcher/document.php?id=cqresrre1991042600.

Goldberg, Harold. 2011. *All Your Base Are Belong to Us: How Fifty Years of Videogames Conquered Pop Culture*. New York: Three Rivers Press.

Grabarczyk, Paweł. 2020. "The Past through Stereoscopic Lenses. Video Games Nostalgia in Virtual Reality." *Przegląd Kulturoznawczy* 2 (44): 54–74. https://doi.org/10.4467/20843860PK.20.014.12378.

Green, Nicola. 1999. "Strange Yet Stylish Headgear VR: Consumption and the Construction of Gender." *Information, Communication & Society* 2 (4): 454–475. https://doi.org/10.1080/136911899359501.

Griffiths, James Alan. 2016. "Bound High." In *Video Games You Will Never Play*, 265–266. Unseen64.

Gunning, Tom. 2012. "Hand and Eye: Excavating a New Technology of the Image in the Victorian Era." *Victorian Studies* 54 (3): 495–516. https://doi.org/10.2979/victorianstudies.54.3.495.

HAL Laboratory. 2001. *Super Smash Bros. Melee*. Nintendo GameCube. Nintendo.

Halverson, Dave. 2004a. "Editor's View." *Play*, volume 3, no. 7, July, 52..

Halverson, Dave. 1995. "Virtual Boy." *GameFan*, volume 3, no. 7, 1995, 56-58.

Halverson, Dave. 2004b. "The Mothers of Invention." *Play*, volume 3, no. 3, 2004, 4.

Hamano, Nobuo, and Kazumi Matsumoto. 1985. Electronic Stereoscopic Viewing Device. US4561723A, issued 1985. https://image-ppubs.uspto.gov/dirsearch-public/print/downloadPdf/4561723

Harris, Blake J. 2014. *Console Wars: Sega, Nintendo, and the Battle That Defined a Generation*. New York: Harper Collins Publishers.

Harrod, Warren. 1997. "Japan Direct." *Official UK Nintendo Magazine*, no. 61, October 1997, 14–15.

Herman, Leonard. 2001. *Phoenix: The Fall & Rise of Videogames*. 3rd ed. Springfield, NJ: Rolenta Press.

Horowitz, Ken. 2018. *The Sega Arcade Revolution*. Jefferson, NC: McFarland & Company.

Hudson Soft. 1995a. *Panic Bomber*. Nintendo of America.

Hudson Soft. 1995b. *Panic Bomber Instruction Booklet*. Hudson Soft.

Hudson Soft. 1995c. *Tobidase! Panibon*. Nintendo.

IGN Staff. 2011. "GDC: 10 Things You Didn't Know about Donkey Kong Country Returns and Retro Studios." *IGN US* (blog). March 3, 2011. https://web.archive.org/web/20150413093922/http://www.ign.com/articles/2011/03/04/gdc-10-things-you-didnt-know-about-donkey-kong-country-returns-and-retro-studios.

Inoue, Osamu. 2010. *Nintendo Magic*. New York: Vertical.

Intelligent Systems and Nintendo EPD. 2018. *WarioWare Gold*. Nintendo 3DS. Nintendo.

Iwata, Satoru. 2011. "2. Shigeru Miyamoto Talks Virtual Boy." *Iwata Asks: Nintendo 3DS* (blog). March 22, 2011. https://www.nintendo.co.uk/Iwata-Asks/Iwata-Asks-Nintendo-3DS/Vol-1-And-That-s-How-the-Nintendo-3DS-Was-Made/2-Shigeru-Miyamoto-Talks-Virtual-Boy/2-Shigeru-Miyamoto-Talks-Virtual-Boy-229419.html.

Jacobson, Linda. 1994. *Garage Virtual Reality*. Indianapolis, IN: Sams. https://archive.org/details/garagevirtualrea00jaco.

Järvinen, Aki. 2002. "Gran Stylissimo: The Audiovisual Elements and Styles in Computer and Video Games." In *Proceedings of Computer Games and Digital Cultures Conference*, edited by Frans Mäyrä, 113–126. Tampere, Finland: Tampere University Press. http://www.digra.org/wp-content/uploads/digital-library/05164.35393.pdf.

Jones, David. 1995. "Save for X-Mas, Skip the R-Zone." *Chicago Tribune*, November 28, 1995. https://www.chicagotribune.com/news/ct-xpm-1995-11-28-9511280045-story.html.

Jones, Steven E., and George K. Thiruvathukal. 2012. *Codename Revolution: The Nintendo Wii Platform*. Platform Studies. Cambridge, MA: MIT Press.

Juul, Jesper. 2019. *Handmade Pixels: Independent Video Games and the Quest for Authenticity*. Cambridge, MA: MIT Press.

Kalinske, Thomas. 2015. "Email from Thomas Kalinske to Benj Edwards," July 31, 2015.

Keizer, Gregg. 1993. "Out-of-House Experiences." *Omni* 16(3): 12.

Kent, Steven L. 2001. *The Ultimate History of Videogames*. Roseville, CA: Prima Publishing.

King, Henry C. 1955. *The History of the Telescope*. Mineola, NY: Charles Griffin/Dover Publications.

Kirby, David A. 2011. "Creating a Techno-Mythology for a New Age: The Production History of the Lawnmower Man." In *Science Fiction and Computing: Essays on Interlinked Domain*, edited by David L. Ferro and Eric G. Swedin, 214–229. McFarland & Company.

Kohler, Chris. 2019. "Luigi's Latest Parody Nintendo Console Is the Best One Yet." *Kotaku* (blog). October 16, 2019. https://kotaku.com/luigis-latest-parody-nintendo-console-is-the-best-one-y-1839072375.

Kr155e. 2010. "Bound High Rom Released!" *Planet Virtual Boy* (blog). May 3, 2010. https://www.virtual-boy.com/forums/t/bound-high-rom-released/.

Kr155e. 2013a. "You'll Enjoy Faceball on Your Virtual Boy Soon!" *Planet Virtual Boy* (blog). January 6, 2013. https://www.virtual-boy.com/forums/t/youll-enjoy-faceball -on-your-virtual-boy-soon/.

Kr155e. 2013b. "Faceball: Remastered out Now." *Planet Virtual Boy* (blog). April 29, 2013. https://www.virtual-boy.com/forums/t/faceball-remastered-out-now/.

Kylearan, dir. 2014. *Ascend by Cluster and DMA*. https://youtu.be/wcCJM7b9EMU.

Lanier, Jaron. 2017. *Dawn of the New Everything: Encounters with Reality and Virtual Reality*. New York: Henry Holt and Company.

Leonard, Brett, dir. 1992. *The Lawnmower Man*. New Line Cinema.

Lin, Judy. 2014. "The Story Behind Shuji Nakamura's Invention of Blue LEDs." *LEDinside* (blog). October 14, 2014. https://www.ledinside.com/news/2014/10/the_story _behind_shuji_nakamuras_invention_of_blue_leds.

Loguidice, Bill, and Matt Barton. 2009. *Vintage Games: An Insider Look at the History of Grand Theft Auto, Super Mario, and the Most Influential Games of All Time*. Burlington, MA: Focal Press.

Magic Eye. 2018. "About Magic Eye." Magic Eye. 2018. https://www.magiceye.com/about/

Makino, Takefumi. 2010a. *Game no chichi Yokoi Gunpei den: Nintendo no DNA wo sozo shita otoko* [The legend of Gunpei Yokoi, the father of games: The man who created the DNA of Nintendo]. Translated by John F. Bukacek. Tokyo, Japan: Kadokawa Shoten.

Makino, Takefumi. 2010b. *Gunpei Yokoi: Vie et philosophie du dieu des jouets Nintendo*. Translated by Florent Gorges. France: Pix'n Love Editions.

Makino, Takefumi. 2015. "Email Sent to Benj Edwards," August 9, 2015.

Marchand, André. 2016. "The Power of an Installed Base to Combat Lifecycle Decline: The Case of Video Games." *International Journal of Research in Marketing* 33 (1): 140–154. https://doi.org/10.1016/j.ijresmar.2015.06.006.

Marchand, André, and Thorsten Hennig-Thurau. 2013. "Value Creation in the Video Game Industry: Industry Economics, Consumer Benefits, and Research Opportunities." *Journal of Interactive Marketing* 27 (3): 141–157. https://doi.org/10.1016 /j.intmar.2013.05.001.

Martin, Brett S. 2018. *Virtual Reality*. Tech Bytes—High Tech. Norwood House Press.

McChoke, Chokey. 2004. "Boktai: The Sun Is in Your Hand." *Hyper*, no. 128, June 2004, 73.

McFerran, Damien. 2019. "Feature: The Game-Changing Nintendo VR Headset That Never Was." *NintendoLife* (blog). November 27, 2019. https://www.nintendolife.com /news/2019/11/feature_the_game-changing_nintendo_vr_headset_that_never_was.

McGowan, Chris. 1995. "Networks Unite Players on Phone Lines." *Billboard*, August 26, 1995, 98.

McTiernan, John, dir. 1985. *Predator*. Twentieth Century Fox.

Mellott, Kevin. 2017. "Link Cable Project Interest—Comment." *Planet Virtual Boy* (blog). July 2, 2017. https://www.virtual-boy.com/forums/t/link-cable-project -interest/page/11/#replies.

Miller, Chuck, F. E. Dille, and Johnny L. Wilson. 1994. "Battle of the New Machines." *Computer Gaming World*, no. 114, January 1994, 64–76.

Miller, D. A. 1990. "Anal Rope." *Representations*, no. 32 (Autumn): 114–133. https:// www.jstor.org/stable/2928797.

M.K. 2017. "Mario's Tennis Multiplayer Patch." *Planet Virtual Boy* (blog). August 5, 2017. https://www.virtual-boy.com/forums/t/mario-s-tennis-multiplayer-patch/.

Mean Machines Sega. 1993. "SEGA VR: The Megadrive Virtual Reality!" no. 10, August 1993, 16–17.

Montfort, N., and I. Bogost. 2009. *Racing the Beam: The Atari Video Computer System*. Platform Studies. Boston, MA: MIT Press.

Mora-Cantallops, M., and I. Bergillos. 2018. "Fan Preservation of 'Flopped' Games and Systems: The Case of the Virtual Boy in Spain." *Catalan Journal of Communication & Cultural Studies* 10 (2): 213–229. https://doi.org/10.1386/cjcs.10.2.213_1.

Moss, Richard. 2022. *Shareware Heroes: The Renegades Who Redefined Gaming at the Dawn of the Internet*. London: Unbound.

Mr. Anonymous. 2013. *Hyper Fighting*. Self Published. https://www.virtual-boy.com/homebrew/hyper-fighting/.

Murphy, Sheila C. 2014. "Controllers." In *The Routledge Companion to Video Game Studies*, edited by Mark J. P. Wolf and Bernard Perron, 19–24. New York and London: Routledge.

N64Pro Staff. 1997. "Karaoke Kontroller?" *N64 Pro*, no. 2, Christmas 1997, 9.

N.E. Thing. 1993. *Magic Eye: A New Way of Looking at the World*. Provincetown, MA: N.E. Thing Enterprises.

Newman, Michael Z. 2015. "The Name of the Game Is Jocktronics: Sport and Masculinity in Early Video Games." In *Playing to Win: Sports, Video Games, and the Culture of Play*, edited by Robert Alan Brookey and Thomas P. Oates, 23–44. Bloomington: Indiana University Press.

Next Generation. 1995a. "An Audience with Gumpei Yokoi." volume 1, no. 4, April 1995, 44–46.

Next Generation. 1995b. "Home VR: Hasbro Turns up the Heat." volume 1, no. 7, July 1995, 24–25.

Next Generation——. 1995c. "Zone Hunter (Review).",October 1995.

Next Generation. 1995d. "Nintendo Pins Hopes on Virtual Boy." volume 1, March 1995, 20–21.

Next Generation. 1995e. "The US Sony PlayStation Has Landed." volume 1, no. 9, 1995, 14–15.

Next Generation. 1995f. "Virtual Reality: The Miracle Technology." volume 1, no. 9, 1995, 36–45.

Next Generation Staff. 1996. "Breaking (Column)." *Next Generation*, volume 2, no. 19, July 1996, 24.

Next Level Games. 2019. *Luigi's Mansion 3*. Nintendo Switch. Nintendo.

Ngai, Sianne. 2020. *Theory of the Gimmick: Aesthetic Judgement and Capitalist Form*. Cambridge, MA: The Belknapp Press of Harvard University Press.

Nicoll, Benjamin. 2019. *Minor Platforms in Videogame History*. Amsterdam, Netherlands: Amsterdam University Press.

Nintendo. 1995a. "'Blockbuster' Launch for Nintendo Virtual Boy." Press Release. http://www.planetvb.com/modules/advertising/?r04.

Nintendo. 1995b. "Nintendo Offers More True 3-D Fun—For Less." Press Release. http://www.planetvb.com/modules/advertising/?r08.

Nintendo. 1995c. "Virtual Boy Advertisement—Caveman." *Next Generation*, volume 1, no. 12, 1995, 106–107.

Nintendo. 1995d. "Virtual Boy Advertisement—Doc Martens." *Next Generation*, volume 1, no. 9, 1995, 120–121.

Nintendo. 1995e. *Virtual Boy Development Manual (NOA-06-8085-001 REV C)*.

Nintendo. 1995f. *Virtual Boy Instruction Booklet*. Nintendo.

Nintendo. 1995g. "Virtual Boy Launch Date Announced." Press Release. http://www .planetvb.com/modules/advertising/?r:

Nintendo, dir. 1995h. "Virtual Boy 'No Escape' US TV Commercial." https://www.youtube .com/watch?v=HapXTgMj11M

Nintendo. 1995i. *Virtual Boy Wario Land Instruction Booklet*. Nintendo.

Nintendo. 1996. "Dragon Hopper (Virtual Boy)." *"Focused on Fun"—1996 E3 Presskit*.

Nintendo. 1999. *Gameboy Development Manual V1.1—DMG-06-4216-001-B*. Nintendo.

Nintendo. 2019. *Nintendo Labo VR Kit*. Nintendo Switch. Nintendo of America.

Nintendo. 2021. "Dedicated Video Game Sales Units." December 31, 2021. https:// www.nintendo.co.jp/ir/en/finance/hard_soft/index.html.

Nintendo EAD. 2013. *Animal Crossing: New Leaf*. Nintendo 3DS. Nintendo.

Nintendo of America. 1995a. "Reflection Technology Joins Nintendo of America at Winter Consumer Electronics Show in Las Vegas." https://www.virtual-boy.com /events/winter-ces-1995/articles/733037/.

Nintendo of America. 1995b. "Nintendo Introduces New Virtual Boy Price; More Games Introduced." https://www.virtual-boy.com/games/virtual-boy-wario-land/articles /733036/.

Nintendo of America. 1996. "'Focused on Fun' E3 1996 Presskit." https://www.virtual -boy.com/events/e3-1996/articles/733033/.

Nintendo Power. 1995a. "Virtual Boy Update." January 1995, 52–53.

Nintendo Power. 1995b. "Virtual Boy Wario Land." no. 79, December 1995, 36–45, 106.

Nintendo Power. 1996a. "Bound High." volume 81, February 1996, 99.

Nintendo Power. 1996b. "Zero Racers: Flat-Out Speed." volume 87, August 1996, 40–41.

Nintendo R&D1. 1995a. *Teleroboxer*. Nintendo.

Nintendo R&D1. 1995b. *Virtual Boy Wario Land*. Nintendo.

Nintendo3DSuk, dir. 2014. *Tomodachi Life Direct Presentation—10.04.2014*. https:// youtu.be/5lQI0UK4SLI?t=130.

Nintendo/NBC/Blockbuster. 1995. "Must See 3-D Sweepstakes Brochure."

Nishino, Hideaki. 2022. "PlayStation VR2 and PlayStation VR2 Sense Controller: The Next Generation of VR Gaming on PS5." *Playstation.Blog* (blog). January 4, 2022. https://blog.playstation.com/2022/01/04/playstation-vr2-and-playstation-vr2 -sense-controller-the-next-generation-of-vr-gaming-on-ps5/.

NobelPrize.org. 2014. "Press Release—The Nobel Prize in Physics 2014." October 7, 2014. https://www.nobelprize.org/prizes/physics/2014/press-release/.

OED Online. 2021. "Gimmick, n." https://www.oed.com/view/Entry/78347?isAdvanced =false&result=1&rskey=MtWMPx&.

Ogata, Amy. 2002. "Viewing Souvenirs: Peepshows and International Expositions." *Journal of Design History* 15 (2): 69–82.

Old!Gamer. 2016. *Super Nintendo: A história completa do melhor videogame da Nintendo*. Vol. 2. São Paulo, Brasil: Europa.

Pallant, Chris. 2011. *Demystifying Disney: A History of Disney Feature Animation*. New York and London: Continuum Books.

Parish, Jeremy. 2021. *Virtual Boy Works*. Raleigh, NC: Limited Run Games.

Patney, Anjul, Marco Salvi, Joohwan Kim, Anton Kaplanyan, Chris Wyman, Nir Benty, David Luebke, and Aaron Lefohn. 2016. "Towards Foveated Rendering for Gaze-Tracked Virtual Reality." *ACM Transactions on Graphics* 35 (6): 1–12. https://doi.org/10.1145/2980179.2980246.

Patterson, Robert. 1992. "Human Stereopsis." *Human Factors* 34 (6): 669–692. https://doi.org/10.1177/001872089203400603.

Perfect, Guy. 2014. "New Article." Reply. *Planet Virtual Boy Forums.* https://www.virtual-boy.com/forums/t/new-article-2/.

Pizza Rolls Royce. 2023. "Porting Virtual Boy Wario Land to the Game Boy Advance." *Medium.com.* January 3, 2023. https://medium.com/@pizzarollsroyce/porting-virtual-boy-wario-land-to-the-game-boy-advance-d7a3c8c1fb7.

Planet Virtual Boy. n.d. "Games." Accessed May 5, 2022. https://www.virtual-boy.com/games/.

Reflection Technology. 1988. "Reflection Technology, Inc. Business Plan January 1988."

Retro Gamer. 2007. "The Future Is Dead: The Rise and Fall of Virtuality." no. 38, May 2007, 72–79.

Rheingold, Howard. 1991. *Virtual Reality.* New York: Summit Books.

Roquet, Paul. 2022. *The Immersive Enclosure: Virtual Reality in Japan.* New York: Columbia University Press.

RPGs For Raccoons, "Nintendo Virtual Boy Commercial 2", Advertisement, *RPGs For Raccoons,* 1995. https://youtu.be/lzSwrHldgok?si=oS8BHW6uzn3k1rDN.

Ryan, Jeff. 2011. *Super Mario: How Nintendo Conquered America.* New York: Portfolio/Penguin.

Salter, Anastasia, and John Murray. 2014. *Flash: Building the Interactive Web.* Cambridge, MA: MIT Press.

Schilling, Melissa. 2003. "Technological Leapfrogging: Lessons from the U.S. Video Game Console Industry." *California Management Review* 45 (3): 6–32.

Schroeder, Ralph. 1995. "Virtual Environments and the Varieties of Interactive Experience in Information and Communication Technologies: An Analysis of Legend Quest." *Convergence* 1 (2): 45–55. https://doi.org/10.1177/135485659500100207.

Sega Pro. 1994. "Arcade News." no. 37, October 1994, 9.

Sega Visions. 1993. "Heavy Equipment: SEGA VR." August/September 1993, 92–93.

Semrad, Ed. 1995. "Insert Coin: Nintendo Stumbles with Virtual Boy Intro." *Electronic Gaming Monthly,* volume 8, no. 1, January 1995, 6.

Sharp, Philip. 2007. "Peep-Boxes to Pixels: An Alternative History of Video Game Space." In *Situated Play, Proceedings of DiGRA 2007 Conference,* 278–285. Tokyo, Japan: DiGRA. http://www.digra.org/wp-content/uploads/digital-library/07312.18290.pdf.

Sheff, David. 1993. *Game Over: How Nintendo Zapped an American Industry, Captured Your Dollars, and Enslaved Your Children.* New York: Random House.

Sheff, David, and Andy Eddy. 1999. *Game Over: Press Start to Continue.* Wilson, CT: GamePress.

Simons, Iain, and James Newman. 2018. *A History of Videogames.* London: Carlton Books.

Sloan, Robin J. 2016. "Nostalgia Videogames as Playable Game Criticism." *GAME* 5: 34–45. https://rke.abertay.ac.uk/files/31605041/Sloan_NostalgiaVideoGames_Published_2016.pdf.

Smith, Alexander. 2020. *They Create Worlds: The Story of the People and Companies That Shaped the Video Game Industry Volume 1: 1971–1982*. Boca Raton, FL: CRC Press.

Sony Interactive Entertainment. 2020. "PlayStation Network Monthly Active Users Reaches 103 Million." *Sony Interactive Entertainment Press Releases* (blog). January 7, 2020. https://www.sie.com/en/corporate/release/2020/200107.html.

Sora Ltd., and Bandai Namco. 2014. *Super Smash Bros. for Wii U*. Nintendo Wii U. Nintendo.

speedyink. 2017. "Link Cable Project Interest—Comment." *Planet Virtual Boy* (blog). August 11, 2017. https://www.virtual-boy.com/forums/t/link-cable-project-interest/page/16/#replies.

Stevens, Benjamin. 2015. "Benjamin Steven's Role in the Making of Hyper Fighting." *Planet Virtual Boy* (blog). February 6, 2015. https://www.virtual-boy.com/forums/t/benjamin-stevens-role-in-the-making-of-hyper-fighting/.

Sutherland, Ivan E. 1968. "A Head-Mounted Three Dimensional Display." In *Proceedings of the December 9–11, 1968 Fall Joint Computer Conference*, 757–764. https://dl.acm.org/doi/pdf/10.1145/1476589.1476686.

Swalwell, Melanie. 2007. "The Remembering and the Forgetting of Early Digital Games: From Novelty to Detritus and Back Again." *Journal of Visual Culture* 6: 255–273.

Szczepaniak, John. 2015. *The Untold History of Japanese Game Developers: Volume 2*. United Kingdom: Createspace.

Taito. 1978. *Space Invaders*. Bally Midway.

Taito. 1979. *Space Invaders Part II*. Taito Corporation.

Taito. 1995. *Space Invaders: Virtual Collection*. Taito Corporation.

Taylor Jr., Ivan O. 2015. "Video Games, Fair Use and the Internet: The Plight of the Let's Play." *University of Illinois Journal of Law, Technology & Policy* 2015 (1): 247–271. https://heinonline.org/HOL/Page?handle=hein.journals/jltp2015&id=249&collection=journals&index=.

Taylor, Laurie N., and Zach Whalen. 2008. "Playing the Past: An Introduction." In *Playing the Past: History and Nostalgia in Video Games*, edited by Zach Whalen and Laurie N. Taylor, 1–15. Nashville, TN: Vanderbilt University Press.

T&E Soft. 1995a. *Golf*. Nintendo of America.

T&E Soft. 1995b. *Golf Instruction Booklet*. Nintendo of America.

T&E Soft. 1995c. *Red Alarm*. Nintendo.

The Lab Rat. 1997. "GamePro Labs: A Player's Guide to Peripherals." *GamePro*, no. 102, March 1997, 30.

The Whizz. 1995. "The Virtual Boy: Better Red." *GamePro*, volume 7, no. 9, 1995, 16–17.

Therrien, Carl, and Martin Picard. 2016. "Enter the Bit Wars: A Study of Video Game Marketing and Platform Crafting in the Wake of the TurboGrafx-16 Launch." *New Media & Society* 18 (10): 2323–2339.

Thomasson, Michael. 2014. "Retrogaming." In *The Routledge Companion to Video Game Studies*, edited by Mark J. P. Wolf and Bernard Perron, 339–344. New York and London: Routledge.

Tobin, Samuel. 2013. *Portable Play in Everyday Life: The Nintendo DS*. New York: Palgrave Macmillan.

RPGs For Raccoons. "Nintendo Virtual Boy Commercial 2", available at https://youtu.be/lzSwrHldgok?si=oS8BHW6uzn3k1rDN.

Verweij, Agnes. 2010. "Perspective in a Box." *Nexus Network Journal* 12 (1): 47–62. https://link.springer.com/content/pdf/10.1007%2F978-3-0346-0518-2.pdf.

VideoGameKraken. n.d. "CyberMaxx by VictorMaxx." *The Video Game Kraken* (blog). Accessed October 12, 2021a. http://videogamekraken.com/cybermaxx-by-victor maxx.

VideoGameKraken. n.d. "StuntMaster by VictorMaxx." *The Video Game Kraken* (blog). Accessed October 12, 2021b. http://videogamekraken.com/stuntmaster-by-victor maxx.

View Askew Productions. 1995. "Mallrats Autostereographic Advertisement." *Next Generation*.

Voskuil, Erik. 2014. *Before Mario: The Fantastic Toys from the Video Game Giant's Early Days*. Montreuil, Paris, France: Omaké Books.

Wade, Nicholas J. 2004. "Philosophical Instruments and Toys: Optical Devices Extending the Art of Seeing." *Journal of the History of the Neurosciences* 13 (1): 102–124. https://doi.org/10.1080/09647040490885538.

Wajda, Shirley, and Kathryn Grover. 1992. "A Room with a Viewer: The Parlor Stereoscope, Comic Stereographs, and the Psychic Role of Play in Victorian America." In *Hard at Play: Leisure in America, 1840–1940*, edited by Kathryn Grover, 112–138. Amherst and Rochester, NY: The University of Massachusetts Press & The Strong Museum.

Watson, Benjamin. 1994. "A Survey of Virtual Reality in Japan." *Presence: Teleoperators and Virtual Environments* 3 (1): 1–18.

Wells, Ben. 2015. "Personal Communication: Telephone Call with Ben Wells by Benj Edwards," July 28, 2015.

Weyer, Martin van de. 2014. "Nintendo, Japan and Longing: Videogames Embodying and Communicating Cultural Desires." Doctoral diss., University of New South Wales, Australia.

Wheatstone, Charles. 1838. "Contributions to the Physiology of Vision.—Part the First. On Some Remarkable, and Hitherto Unobserved, Phenomena of Binocular Vision." In *Philosophical Transactions of the Royal Society of London*, 371–394. https://doi.org/10.1098/rstl.1838.0019

White, H. C. 1895. Stereoscope. US548148A, filed 1895, and issued October 15, 1895.

Willumsen, Ea Christina, and Milan Jaćević. 2019. "A Typology of Rumble." In *Proceedings of the 2019 DiGRA Conference*. DiGRA. http://www.digra.org/wp-content/uploads/digital-library/DiGRA_2019_paper_821.pdf.

Wittenhagen, Jeffrey. 2019. *The Complete Virtual Boy*. Hagen's Alley Entertainment.

Wolf, Mark J. P. 2008a. "Arcade Games of the 1970s." In *The Video Game Explosion: A History from Pong to PlayStation and Beyond*, edited by Mark J. P. Wolf, 35–44. Westport, CT: Greenwood Press.

Wolf, Mark J. P. 2008b. "Laserdisc Games." In *The Video Game Explosion: A History from Pong to PlayStation and Beyond*, edited by Mark J. P. Wolf, 99–102. Westport, CT: Greenwood Press.

Wolf, Mark J. P. 2009. "Z-Axis Development in the Video Game." In *The Video Game Theory Reader 2*, edited by Bernard Perron and Mark J. P. Wolf, 151–168. New York: Routledge.

Yokoi, Gunpei, Ichiro Shirai, Kenichi Sugino, and Noburo Wakitani. 1997. 保持具 (Holder). JPH0943535A, filed July 25, 1995, and issued February 14, 1997. https://patents.google.com/patent/JPH0943535A/.

Yokoi, Gunpei, and Takefumi Makino. 2010. *Yokoi Gunpei Game Kan RETURNS: Game Boy wo unda hassoryoku* [The Yokoi Gunpei Museum RETURNS: The creative power which gave rise to Game Boy]. Translated by John F. Bukacek. Tokyo, Japan: Film Art Co.

Youngblut, Christine, Rob E. Johnston, Sarah H. Nash, Ruth A. Wienclaw, and Craig A. Will. 1996. "Review of Virtual Environment Interface Technology." IDA Paper P-3186. Alexandria, VA: Institute for Defense Analysis. https://apps.dtic.mil/sti /pdfs/ADA314134.pdf.

Zachara, Matt, and José P. Zagal. 2009. "Challenges for Success in Stereo Gaming: A Virtual Boy Case Study." In *Proceedings of the International Conference on Advances in Computer Entertainment Technology*, 99–106. Athens, Greece: ACM. https://dl .acm.org/doi/pdf/10.1145/1690388.1690406.

Zone, Ray. 2007. *Stereoscopic Cinema and the Origins of 3-D Film*. Lexington: The University Press of Kentucky.

Index